Flow

An Illuminated Training Manual

How to Thrive in Love, Work, and Play

Flow

An Illuminated Training Manual

How to Thrive in Love, Work, and Play

Steven Budden

Sparrowdown Press
Oakland, CA

First Print Edition USA 2013

ISBN-13: 978-1481293266

ISBN-10: 1481293265

A mountain keeps an echo deep inside itself.
That's how 1 hold your voice.

1 am scrap wood thrown into your fire,
and quickly reduced to smoke.

1 saw you and became empty.
This emptiness, more beautiful than existence,
it obliterates existence, and yet when it comes,
existence thrives and creates even more existence!

To praise is to praise
how one surrenders
to the emptiness.

-Rumi

Table of Contents

DEDICATIONS   13
ACKNOWLEDGEMENTS   17
HOW I NEARLY BECAME ONE OF THE INVISIBLE   19
A DASH OF CONTEXT   23
TRANSMISSION OF THE ART OF BEING   25
1. BODY AWARENESS TRACKING   27
2. THE MIND IS A STILL POOL   28
UNTANGLING THE BODY MIND COMPLEX   29
WHO AM I?   33
FLUIDITY: THE LIQUID UNDERSTANDING   37
FLUIDITY: WITH EASE AND FLOW   41
1. MORNING SUPER HYDRATION PRACTICE   45
2. HOMEMADE SACRED WATER   45
A RIVER OF ENERGY RUNS THROUGH US   47
IMAGINATION IS NOT DISTINCT FROM REALITY   49
WORDS CREATE, WORDS DESTROY   53
EMOTIONS AS THE KEY TO HAPPINESS AND FULFILLMENT
                                                         57
SWEEP THE MIND WITH BREATH   59
1. ABDOMINAL BREATHING   60
FIXING THE UNBROKEN   61
THE CHAKRAS: HOW WE PLUG INTO THE MATRIX   63
LOVE & GRATITUDE: OUR HIGHEST VIBRATION   65
1. GRATITUDE JOURNALING   65
FIRST, LOVE THYSELF   67
1. MIRROR MIRROR ON THE WALL: 68
ENERGETIC AMPUTATIONS   71
1. SELF LOVE BODY SCAN   71
AFFIRMATIONS: WINDOWS TO THE UNCONSCIOUS   73
FEAR: DEVOURER OF LOVE   75
1. FACING FEAR EXERCISE   78
GROUND ZERO: BIRTH TRAUMA   79

WHY BIRTH LEAVES SUCH A POWERFUL IMPRINT   **81**

AN IMMACULATE CONCEPT - MY BIRTH   **83**

1. BIRTH RESEARCH- REDISCOVER YOUR ROOTS   85

CELLS: WELCOME TO THE HOLOGRAM   **87**

WE ARE GRACE, EMBODIED   **89**

NON-VIOLENT COMMUNICATION   **91**

1. I FEEL BECAUSE I NEED   94

FOOD AS VIBRATION   **97**

WE CANNOT LIVE ON BREAD ALONE   **101**

1. LEMONADE MATRIX CLEARING   103

2. BLESSING FOOD   104

SKIN – WHAT CONNECTS US   **107**

DEATH BECOMES US   **109**

1. REHEARSE YOUR DEATH   110

2. SAY THE UNSAID   110

3. LITTLE DEATHS   111

CLEARING TRAUMA: RELEASING OLD WAYS OF BEING **113**

THE PHYSIOLOGY OF TRAUMA   **115**

THE SACRED METAMORPHOSIS   **117**

AWAKENING THE LIGHT BODY   **119**

OUR BODIES KNOW MORE THAN WE DO   **121**

THE LIFE GIVING SUN   **123**

RELATIONSHIPS AND THE MEANING OF LIFE   **125**

THE FULL MOON, FASTING INTO SANITY   **129**

1. FAST AT THE FULL MOON   130

HOLISTIC VISION: WINDOWS TO THE SOUL   **131**

1. VISION AWARENESS EXERCISE   134

BE THE CHANGE   **137**

CHASING BUDDHA   **139**

SEX AND SACRED INTIMACY   **143**

1. BIODYNAMIC CENTERING PRACTICE   147

2. WHITE TANTRIC GAZE   148

SOUL CONTRACTS: UNLOCKING THE SACRED MYSTERY OF LOVE   **151**

FLUIDITY IN LOVE   **155**

PAIN AS THE PATH TO JOY   157
LUCY AND HER FATHER   159
FEET: OUR ENERGETIC ROOTS   161
1.   FLUID STANDING TUTORIAL   162
2.   BAREFOOT AWARENESS PRACTICE   163
HUGS AND THE LURE OF HUMAN CONNECTION   165
WHEN I WAS A HEADLESS MONK   167
TRANSFORMING THE MUNDANE INTO SACRED RITUAL:
THE POWER OF IMAGINATION   171
FLUID MOVEMENT   173
THE SUBTLE ART OF THRIVING   175
CONCLUSION   176
A PENULTIMATE REQUEST   177
ABOUT THE AUTHOR   178

The Chakras

Seventh Chakra
Sahasrara "Thousand Petaled- The Unqualified Absolute"
Location: At the top of the skull.
Lessons related to Spirituality
Key: Live in the present moment
Color: Violet or White or Gold **Element:** None **Seed Sound:** Visarga

Sixth Chakra
Ajna "The Qualified Absolute"
Location: In the center of the skull at the forehead just between the eyes.
Lessons related to mind, intuition, insight, and wisdom
Key : Seek only the Truth
Color: Indigo **Element:** Mahat (Supreme element which contains the essence of all elements) **Seed Sound:** Aum

Fifth Chakra
Vishuddha "Purified"
Location: At the spine behind the throat.
Lessons related to will and self expression
Key: Surrender Personal Will to Divine Will
Color: Blue **Element:** Akasha (Ether) **Seed Sound:** Hang

Fourth Chakra
Anahata "The Pure Sound of Creation"
Location: At the spine behind the heart.
Lessons related to love, forgiveness, and compassion
Key: Love is Divine Power
Color: Green **Element:** Air **Seed Sound:** Yang

Third Chakra
Manipura "City of the Shining Jewel"
Location: At the spine behind the solar plexus.
Lessons related to ego, personality, and self-esteem
Key: Honor Oneself **Color:** Yellow **Element:** Fire

Second Chakra
Svadisthana "Her Special Abode"
Location: At the spine just below the navel.
Lessons related to sexuality, work, and physical desire
Key: Honor One Another
Color: Orange **Element:** Water **Seed Sound:** Vang

First Chakra
Muladhara "Root Support"
Location: At the base of the coccyx or tail bone.
Lessons related to the material world
Key: All is One
Color: Red **Element:** Earth **Seed Sound:** Lang

Figure 1

Dedications

• • •

This book is dedicated to she who made it possible, she who inspired its completion, and to the little voice that delivered the words so completely and fearlessly into my life.

"Three things cannot be long hidden: the sun, the moon, and the truth." - Buddha

Acknowledgements

· · ·

I would like to acknowledge you for your persistence and dedication on your journey to wholeness. It thrills me to witness.

Leah Mercado, thank you for believing I was a flower when I felt folded in a bud, and for your radiant authenticity and courage in choosing to celebrate the full spectrum of the human experience.

Mariella Mcroberts, you beautiful thing. Thank you for opening your world to me and for seeing me through a tumultuous year.

David Ross, thank you for illuminating a path to compassion that appealed to my logical mind and for providing an unwavering example of integrity.

Patricia Cramer, thank you for your profound faith in the healing of humanity and your generous contributions to the healing arts.

Jason Calhoun, thank you for bringing so much joy and laughter into my life for so many years. I look forward to the next phase.

Samanvitha Rao, thank you for standing beside me, always, and for asking me questions that penetrated to the essence of life. My version of the answers are in this book.

Amanda Wong, there is no one I would rather meditate beside in the rain on the cusp of a new era. Thank you for being so luminous, so brave, and so free.

Karen Chung, thank you for fearlessly integrating such profound awareness, and for continually reminding me to revere the teeming powers of the imagination.

Rosalyn Fay, words fail me. Thank you for being you.

Teresa Shen, as your chakras unfold, so do mine. Thank you for inspiring me, in your way, to complete this work.

C.B., thank you for your courage to connect even in the face of adversity, and for a summer I won't soon forget.

Chi Nguyen, thank you for courageously pursuing your passions and relentlessly following your truth. It has been inspiring to watch you grow and to grow beside you.

I am so honored to know each and every one of you.

Riley and Sofia, as you bloom, may you never lose touch with your sense of wonder.

To my family, past, present, and future, I love you all, forever.

I would like to give a special thanks to the World School of Massage and Holistic Healing Arts for helping me transform my life, and for teaching fluid ways of being, and for introducing me to a host of kindred spirits.

To all of my friends and loved ones, those known and unknown, my heart is in these pages, and I am grateful to open it in your direction.

How I Nearly Became One of the Invisible

• • •

As I descended hopelessly downward, I saw a very faint light glowing in the distant darkness. My epiphanies have not been conventionally dramatic, but slow and methodical. It was out of desperation I began to learn what I am going to share with you. I was broke, ill, tired, nearly homeless, and lonely even in the company of friends and family. My love affairs were tempestuous and agonizing. I often sank into depression for no apparent reason and struggled even to survive. Life felt like a series of catastrophes that drove me to the brink of... well...

For the next few years, I scoured the depths of various traditions, tore through vast tomes and poured over little dog-eared booklets. My body as my alchemical laboratory, I put myself through any number of strict physical regimens. I leapt across religions and timelines without decorum. I read books by enlightened saints and books by people that toed the line of insanity.

I became like a man possessed on a search for truth and power. I was lost and found more times than I care to remember. The quest was getting... dangerous.

I was enlightened on a beach in Northern California in 2005. I was walking along the strand with my father on the tail end of a coastal road trip. A beautiful woman ran by us, her silken hair waving in her wake. I marveled at her anatomy, the curves of her form. For a moment I wondered if that feeling was lust or a celebration of god's work. I dropped my eyes to the sand, where the imprints of her sneakers followed her into the distance. Suddenly, a Pacific wave washed up onto the shore, and when it swept back out to sea, the footprints were gone. I was washed over with a profound sense of serenity and deep love.

What I experienced there had not been contained in books, though books illuminated the pathway to it. I saw it all in an instant; the ecstasy and the agony; the bliss and the pain; life and death. Nothing was missing and everything was perfect exactly as it was.

Over the next few months, as I struggled to integrate my new awareness, it slowly slipped away again. Though I stumbled back into prior illusions, life was not the same. Once it is seen, the truth, it cannot be unseen.

And then I was in San Diego in 2008, lying on a body board, drifting in Pacific bliss. I'd been catching waves all day, and felt a deep, profound connection with the waters. I was just so grateful to be living in this paradise. One more wave, I thought. A celebratory gesture, then I'll head in.

Even as I had that thought, I could sense a momentous shift. The sound of the waves dropped away. I didn't quite paddle fast enough, or my timing was off, or the universe was trying to tell me something. I had a flash forward. It is difficult to describe because I was now outside of the time matrix. But I knew, somehow I knew what was about to happen. This was my choice. The wave took up the back of the board and before I could even react, I was hurtled against the ocean floor.

I was underwater for a while, rolling around in the sand. I could die here, I thought. The blow to my head was so hard I had the vague feeling that I could be paralyzed, or worse. Maybe I already was dead. If so, it wasn't so bad. I considered going to sleep. I was tired, sick, hopeless. I know I was in the ocean, inundated with salt water, but I remember crying. There was this woman in my life. She just relocated from Los Angeles to be with me. She needed me. And my youngest brother lived with me. He was just coming into his own as a man.

This wasn't my death. This was a wake up call. I woke up and clawed my way toward the light, gasping for air. I rose up and stumbled to shore. The CT scan would say that my 5th cervical vertebra was cracked.

"If you weighed 5 pounds more," the doctor said, "You'd probably be dead or paralyzed. You're very lucky." Tears trickled out of my eyes again. I was 5 days into a water fast and probably weighed 8 pounds less than usual. Serendipitous, I thought.

Thank you, Universe, for continually keeping me in contact with the truth. I have one request; can the reminders in the future be a little gentler?

I wrote this because I don't want you to have to wait for a stroke of luck or a near death experience to illuminate your pathway to joy. I'm going to show you how to build a ladder and climb to heaven with your own body, from wherever you are.

I spent many years drifting aimlessly and took a very convoluted and circuitous route to reach where I am now. Hopefully what I am showing you is a more direct path. Though, honestly, we are each on our road, and if yours is a long and winding one, celebrate every twist and turn. This is life.

A Dash of Context

• • •

2012 was the most tumultuous, terrifying, and transformative year of my life. Paradigms shifted, consciousness exploded, and everything I thought that I knew... well... was tested. Stepping out of the year, I notice that I am not the same man I was when I stepped in. We cannot step into the same river twice, I remind myself. The waters are constantly shifting in a dynamic, liquid dance. Us too. We are, after all, mostly water.

I completed an intensive holistic life coaching program, unfolded stories of my birth and death, lost my lover to a woman, was cast out, dismantled, rebuilt, sexed, purged, cleansed, healed. I felt dark magic, light magic, lived in my car, saw my father break down and wind up in prison, lost my dog. I would have survived, endured, but I probably would not have been able to perform this little piece of alchemical magic if it weren't for the community of kindred spirits that came out of the woodwork around me.

I've wanted to write this book for many years. The story was that I needed just a little bit more. An inexplicable piece was missing. In 2012, life delivered, and absolutely never in the ways that I expected. I learned quickly that flow is not about expectation, but about openness.

I want you to know that I love you, and that the source of all life loves us, and that we live in a safe and loving universe, you and I. There is nothing under the sun that can harm us when we are putting out a vibration of love and gratitude. We are beloved of higher powers. We have spent thousands of years slowly vibrating out of touch with this reality, and now we are finally waking up. It is beautiful to witness, and even more beautiful to experience.

As seekers, saints, mystics, and mortals, we are reclaiming our ancient role as guardians and custodians of the Earth. We all know how to suffer, ail, and die. This book is about remembering how to thrive, celebrate, and ascend. That potential is still encoded in our scrambled DNA (our "junk" DNA).

This book is about expressing our full potential, dropping disempowering "stories" about our limitations, and reclaiming the life of joy and love that is our birthright.

In each moment, out of the infinite network of possible realities, there are really only two options; love or fear, and two choices, acceptance or resistance. Everything else flows from those.

"To fear love is to fear life, and those who fear life are already three parts dead."
- Bertrand Russell

Though I've read widely, I've approached this book from the perspective of the poet. Great poets and artists access their inner wisdom and know. Scientists seek to prove what the poets already knew. A beautiful dialogue ensues.

Though I have included some references where applicable, my goal is to touch you in another place: your heart. And if we resonate together, if even for a moment, our time will not have been spent in vain.

There is nothing in these pages that I have not experienced first hand. I would never espouse a technique simply because it appealed to my logical mind.

What you are about to experience, I have lived; the agony and the ecstasy; the joy and the sorrow. There are other techniques I am still testing on myself. Perhaps I will share those later.

May you find value and guidance here, there, and everywhere.

Transmission of the Art of Being

• • •

Have you noticed that in between the sounds, the thoughts, and the experiences, there is a still place of pure being, where we touch our self-adoring essence?

Have you allowed yourself to enter this sacred space?

Entering this space of pure "being," even for limited durations, sends a powerful, transformative message. The only thing that many spiritual masters throughout history ever did was revel in pure "being." On some level, there is nothing else to do. This is the origin of wisdom. As we enter this sacred space, the energetic systems come into balance. We heal. We thrive. As we come into the present moment, we regain access to the wealth of human potential that most fritter away; sending it scurrying off into the future in the form of hopes and worries, and into the past in the form of regret.

In the moment a human being, fully present, can move mountains, if mountains need to be moved.

Letting go of the typical linear model of time, the frantic urge to "do," is like exorcising a mind possessed. The release is often euphoric, and the world opens up to become a realm of pure possibility.
As S. Suzuki famously stated:

"In the beginner's mind there are many possibilities. In the expert's mind, there are few."
This state can be "transmitted" to another in a variety of ways. This is sometimes called Satori or Enlightenment. It comes as the ego dies little deaths. (The ego, though, is tenacious).

Zen Buddhism is my favorite tradition in this regard.

Nobushige, a great samurai, sought out Hakuin and asked:

"Is there really a heaven and a hell?"

"Who are you?" asked Hakuin.

"I am a samurai," Nobushige replied.

"You?" Hakuin snorted. "What lord would employ you? You look like a beggar!"

A furious Nobushige began to draw his sword.

"Here open the gates of hell," Hakuin said, calmly.

Nobushige, moved by Hakuin's calm stature and seemingly endless courage, began to sheath his sword.

"Here open the gates of heaven," said Hakuin.
Nobushige, dazzled, bowed in reverence.

Zen master Hakuin, who wrote a beautiful autobiography, had mastered present moment awareness, and in doing so he mastered human communication. The two go hand in hand. He was able to speak from the heart, and come from a place of love that wasn't clouded with fear, even under threat of a samurai's sword. His journey didn't require any esoteric chanting or convoluted doctrines. Hakuin just sat there and learned to distinguish the "self" from the flood of thoughts that often assail us. He just sat and basked in that stillness, until the sacred space of "being" opened up to him. Rather, until he opened up to it.

The above example, adapted from Zen Flesh and Zen Bones, is a favorite of mine because it shows how a fearless Hakuin nonviolently transformed Nobushige, who had lived a lifetime of cultivated violence, in one lesson. It is about living in integrity and carrying that integrity like a mighty, impenetrable shield. (Gandhi is another powerful example of this principle).

Hakuin, through his awareness, was able to gauge exactly what to say to the mighty samurai. He knew exactly why the samurai approached him, and without "thinking" of a response, he was able to "demonstrate" a response through action-less action.

Perhaps you've heard the adage "Actions speak louder than words?" Actually, what is transformative is the vibration of an action or a word. Actions give off powerful vibrations because they can transcend language. According to the Buddha, it isn't the action itself that determines the karmic consequence of that action, but the underlying intent. Actions stemming from greed, lust, or delusion sow negative karma. Actions stemming from love, gratitude, and compassion sow positive karma.

Our lives are created around us by the power of our vibration. Certain things weaken our vibration and certain things strengthen it. Our vibration is beyond space and time, but it radiates from our physiology in the present moment. Being present increases the frequency of our vibration like nothing else. Hakuin died hundreds of years ago, but his vibration was so powerful that it broke the levee and overflowed the bounds of time to touch us even in the here and now.

Training Suggestions:

1. Body Awareness Tracking

Stand and take a deep breath. As you close your eyes, start to notice physical sensations as they arise in you. There is so much happening within us in each moment. As we tune into our bodies, we can access these subtle body cues.

For a few moments, just follow your attention as it leaps from sensation to sensation in your physical body.

Name the area where you feel the sensation. It might sound like "Big toe, ear lobe, eye, elbow, finger, nose, nostril, belly, thigh, little toe." It doesn't need to be that specific. You know which body part and which sensation you are referring to and that is all that matters.

This awareness practice is training for engaging the present moment. Observing without judgment is the gateway, and it is often simplest to begin with our own sensations. Notice your mind if it tends to wander, or decides to create a story around a sensation. Allow these thoughts to rise and fall, and continue to track sensations as they flow through you.

Thank you David Ross and the Creation Course for introducing me to this technique.

2. The mind is a still pool

Close your eyes and visualize a pool of water in your mind's eye. Every time a thought arises, imagine a droplet of water breaking the surface of the pond and sending out ripples. Continue this until the drips slowly stop coming, and the water becomes still. This meditation gives the compulsive mind something to do while it sinks into an empowered trance state.

This is a beautiful and effective meditation for those of us who are intimidated by the thought of meditation; by all of the mystical talk around it.

Continue for anywhere from a few minutes to half an hour. We can also use this technique when we are triggered. As long as the trigger is not too severe, the mind will soon settle and we can reach out in grace, equanimity, and poise instead of lashing out in anger or desperation.

Untangling The Body Mind Complex

• • •

The brain is the physical organ encased in the skull that seems to drive our responses and house certain memories. The position of the mind is less specific. Did you know that cells throughout the body are imprinted with cellular memory? This is why we can palpate a certain body part and give rise to memories about an injury to that part. Sometimes, something happens that our conscious mind is not ready to fully "feel." We go out of our bodies and store the memories away for future processing. Over time, they trickle out as the conscious and unconscious mind allow.

The heart actually contains neurotransmitters similar to brain cells, and emits a greater vibrational frequency than any other organ, (500 times greater than the brain, in fact).
We have been programmed to think of the intellect as the key resource that humans possess. It is, we have been taught, what sets us apart from animals. The truth is, thoughts are valuable, but we have been blessed with a guidance system that can always ensure that we are in vibrational harmony with our greatest good. It is called our "emotions."

As we track our emotions moment to moment, it becomes possible to continually calibrate our lives so that we are always vibrating in greater and greater alignment.

Since emotional cues are always arising from our body, present moment bodily awareness is one key to living a joyous and productive life. Those trained in eastern religions know this.

Many of us live a head-centered existence. When we make decisions purely from our head, we lose touch with who we are and what we are capable of. We make decisions that "make sense" logically but do nothing to fulfill our purpose or satiate our need for passion. Sometimes everything appears perfect on paper, but it goes against our instinct, for instance; it goes against the grain of our being .

I have discovered, forgotten and rediscovered, over many years and with much resistance, that living a heart-centered life is the key to joy.

The heart is the first organ to form in the fetus. We literally evolve as physical beings around our heart, and to continually evolve we can learn to keep the heart as the center of our being.

When we are in a state of heart-centered awareness, the universe conspires in our favor. When we stumble out of our hearts, we focus on obstacles and competition. The Institute of Heartmath has produced beautiful research on this topic.

The heart is pulsing, emanating, palpable life. We can ignore its aching, or follow it into bliss.

Whether we live out of our heart or our head can also be ascertained by the way we carry ourselves through the world. Our hips, our heart, and our head were designed to be held in one vertical line.

Do we lead with our hips, and fall back with our heart as a safety measure? If so, we may tend to attract and create relationships based on security and sex. Do we lead with our head, or lift our chin to break the connection to our body? If so, we may tend to attract relationships that make sense logically but are devoid of passion.

These physiological clues are signs that somewhere along the way we left a portion of our body in the past. Our bodies contain everything we'll ever need to know about who we are and where we've been.

Living out of the heart is a spiritual practice, but it is also a physical practice. Instead of allowing our chests to cave in, we can lift them proudly, stand in our power, and create space for energy to flow. The next time you are sad or deeply moved, see if you can remain exquisitely aware of what your heart does; whether it opens to revel in the feeling, or collapses in a vain attempt to numb itself. If we use strategies to dull the ache in our heart, it will arise somewhere else in the body.

My own strategy used to be to come into my head in moments of emotional charge and recall some philosophical doctrine or run through a poem about the nature of sadness. I was essentially throwing the mind a bone so it had something to chew on. My body was riddled with aches.

Now, when powerful emotions arise, I relocate into a heart-centered place, imagine breath filling that space. Sometimes I touch it with my hands, to feel it throb and to ground myself. I breathe through it all.

I cry a little more now, I confess, but I also love more.

Who am I?

...

Perhaps divulging a little about my journey might shed a little light on these themes and why I created this work.

I am another soul incarnated in human form. My energy body carries the memories from lifetimes prior, which creep around in the peripheries of my vision. I've been a warrior, a monk, an artist, a saint, a father, a gardener, a healer, a lover, a lion; and probably a myriad of other wonders that I have no conscious recollection of.

In this life I grew up in Arizona, under vast desert skies. I would often look up and gawk into the yawning abyss and yearn. This was filling me up with "space" for possibilities. In Tibetan Shamanism, meditating on one of the five elements replenishes that element in the body and spirit. So perhaps I grew up with an overabundance of "space" and a shortage of "water." Perhaps this is why, when I learned about fluid ways of being, (via Tai Chi, a Tibetan Monk, and World School of Holistic Healing Arts) and I was shattered and transformed.

I was a precocious child. I seemed to excel at literature and the arts. When I was young, I tried to out paint Picasso and out scribe Thoreau. I am amazed now at my audacity then, but is that amazement inherited programming designed to limit human potential?

I was clearly right brain dominant out of the gate (the spiritual, creative side of the brain) and the system (left brain dominant schooling) cooled that fever and tipped the scales to the left. As I navigated this metamorphosis and created beautiful artwork, I worked myself into a foamy frenzy of depression.

I grew up with an inherent knowledge of the "holistic" connection between all aspects of life, but I seemed to forget it intentionally now and then. I looked for love and fulfillment in other people. I toyed with the idea of romance as my only salvation. Mostly I just fantasized about beautiful girls and hyperventilated in their presence.

In my early twenties, a kindred spirit and I traveled to France to study our favorite painters and their environments. Matisse, Van Gogh, and Picasso were my idols at the time. Van Gogh for me symbolized someone who followed his passion wholeheartedly and suffered for it. I am still clearing that program from my consciousness and body.

While I studied painting as a philosophical and spiritual practice, earning my MFA at the San Francisco Art Institute, I went to the limits of "doing" and wondered what it had to do with "being." Where did the two overlap? The artists that epitomized creating out of a state of being were the Zen artists. They meditated in their temples and whipped out brushes now and then to create masterworks. And why, I wondered, did our so-called "perfect" beings never create (Jesus, Buddha, Socrates)? Creation must be some mystical attempt to tip the scales against chaos. If there was no chaos within, then art was superfluous. Which is perhaps why Kierkegaard once wrote, "Poetry may be an ethical diversion." Or do we only see them as "perfect" because we don't have access to their own words (they've been mythologized)?

As I obsessed over painting and creating a reputation, my health deteriorated. Being and doing were conflicting again. Doing was painting nude women in a room saturated with turpentine, noxious fumes on the air. Being was gawking lovingly at the California coast, watching the sunlight ripple off of the water in blinding glints of white, serenaded by the wailing gulls.

But a crisis is a beautiful thing. It lets us know when we have needs that aren't being met.

I embarked on a journey of self-healing and self-discovery, tepidly at first, and then wholeheartedly. I tried a seemingly endless litany of diets, spiritual practices, fasts and cleanses, philosophies, mantras, affirmations, fitness routines. Nothing proved "perfect." I was still looking for salvation from some external source.

Eventually, by borrowing tiny gems from each pool, I was able to rise out of the ashes of despair and empower myself to begin consciously directing my own thoughts and creating my own life. Many of the most powerful techniques and understandings that were delivered to me are contained within these pages.

I am endlessly grateful for my transformation. My vision, which was once unreliable, has become clear and vibrant; my romantic relationships, which verged on emotionally abusive, are now fulfilling and passionate; my financial situation, which was once tenuous and stressful, is now bustling with energy; and I am no longer crippled by the depression and anxiety that used to greet me every morning when I woke. I live and act out of love. I have created a fulfilling career and a business that fills me with inspiration, contribution, and a sense of purpose.

My life is the fruit of my journey thus far, and what I've included in these pages are the seeds that I used.

May they grow within you.

Fluidity: The Liquid Understanding

• • •

Are we solid, stacked bones and flesh? A brittle, eggshell skull propped atop a whimsical column of bone? Think again.

Newborn babies are 78 percent water. By one year of age, this percentage drops to about 65 percent. Blood is 92 percent water. The brain and muscles are about 75 percent water. Fat is only 10 percent water.

Even the bones, which are about 22 percent water, never touch one another. They are buffered by fluid mediums, and they can ebb and flow like a tide. We often learn of anatomy from plastic skeletons or, if we are fortunate, bleached human bones. These beautiful specimens are only the relics, the ghosts of what they once were. In life, bones flex and move, pulse and twist, send out a flurry of cells as needed and release and absorb minerals like sponges.

Fluidity for me means flowing like a river through time. The mind flows from moment to moment; emotions flow in and out of our experience; our bodily fluids are abundant and flow; our creativity leaps from theme to theme with boundless passion; we are flexible in flesh, mind, and spirit; our idea of the body matches its fluid essence; energy flows through our organs and limbs like a stream trickling down a mountain.

Before there was flesh, there was energy. Whether we see this as an allegory of the spirit or more literally as the life force in the sperm meeting the life force of the egg does not matter much here. The body is a network of energy and flesh, and consciousness coalesces around it so that we can interface with the energy all around us. This is called "being." The most essential conduit of our universal life force, the essence of being, is the fluid in and around our cells.

We are not distinct from the energy of the creatures around us. Everything from squirrels, to insects, to birds, to ghosts, to angels inhabit our reality. Those are just words, which help connect abstractions through understanding. But we are all connected on an even deeper level.

Human beings are blessed to be one of the higher life forms in the universe. Our ancient birthright, in the lore of many of the oldest cultures on Earth, is that we are custodians, guardians of the planet. The Earth, a living, pulsing, breathing entity, needs protection and love too.

The universe is, like a symphony, a network of vibration woven together by a variety of instruments. Everything is vibration, even us, the instruments. There are particles that continuously spiral all around us. If we look toward the sky, about 12 inches form our face, sometimes you can see them as white specs flittering in and out of existence in circular patterns. These are the particles of potentiality and the building blocks for manifestation. They dance under our gaze; delight at our attention. As we send out a thought, they begin to move to manifest it before we even speak. But it takes time. Usually thoughts of what we want are so fleeting that there isn't ample time.

Before we were born into this human body, we were spirits or soul force; a type of energy that we can't exactly fathom with our predominant left brain awareness. But when we experience "flow" states or glimpses of enlightenment, the hemispheres of our brain harmonize and we are in direct contact with this source energy.

As souls, or disembodied energy, we chose the circumstances that we would incarnate into. We choose our race, our gender, our status, and our families. We choose the life lessons that would allow us to evolve as souls, and then created a perfect structure around us through which to learn those lessons. So though it may seem like we are victims, we are not. Our "circumstances" were a choice. There are no accidents.

Our greatness depends on how we process and use the situation we've created for our own growth.

This is the general structure of the reality we inhabit. Any illusions of us being "victims" to circumstances are merely that... illusions.

Since we chose to incarnate into physical bodies to learn certain lessons, our resistance to learning those lessons creates blockage. Sometimes we are born with blockage, weighted down with the baggage of past life trauma or birth trauma. Other times, we create blockage in our lives by holding onto that which no longer serves us. Once we make it across the river, it makes no sense to continue to carry our boat through the desert. After things have fulfilled their purpose in our lives, we can release them, lightly and easily, without a feeling of loss. This is as true for physical objects as it is for emotional clinging. When we cling to relics of the past, such as trauma, books, antiques, etc, the weight of those artifacts drags us out of the present moment.

Personally, I believe that it is the human birthright to experience joy and bliss. I had read this a hundred, a thousand times. It held little sway over me until I experienced it first hand during a tremulous, almost accidental wavering of my ego. This experience, which I call "enlightenment" for lack of a better term, felt comprehensively joyous, unfathomably simple, and distinctly ordinary. Every time I feel how pervasive it is, how unassuming, how attainable, I laugh.

Ease is flow, and dis-ease is a lack of flow.

When we are fluid, emotions pass through us. We feel them fully and we move on. We can undergo injuries, being mortal, but chronic trauma does not latch onto our bodies the way it does when we are in a state of resistance. Feeling fully is a key to fluidity. When intense pain or pleasure flood in, we breathe and let our hearts, souls, and bodies tremble and quake, instead of grinding our teeth and holding our breath, waiting for this to pass. "This" is life. Waiting for it to pass?

Flow is also tangled up in movement. Even the breath is a rising and falling. When there is fluid movement, there is life. We move from moment to moment. Emotion is mostly "motion." As Tony Robbins says, "The more you move, the more you feel."

Observing animals in their fluidity can teach us a lot about life. After a fight or a traumatic experience, they shake and vibrate to release the trauma from their tissues, and they move on. Animals don't seem to hold on to trauma like we do. If we have pets, sometimes they even release trauma for us, if we are not doing it for ourselves. Sometimes we hold onto trauma for them by personifying them.

Our state of mind seems to effect whether we will sustain energetic damage when we are physically or emotionally injured. People in a positive state of mind sustain injuries that heal without energetic scars or further complications. Their life force is flowing and the cycle of healing never even pauses to wait for the injury.

When we are in a negative state of mind, damage inflicted can send an energy vector into the surrounding tissues and organs, creating complications down the road. This is a theory espoused by John Upledger in Somatoemotional Release, which I joyfully resonate with.

In this model, we come into this life to flow back into fluidity. Blockages are us carrying the past as trauma, from either this life or a previous one. As we release these blockages, we are free to live the life we've been destined for.

Fluidity: With Ease and Flow

• • •

Vibration flutters through fluid mediums and our body is essentially a matrix of fluid mediums. One fluid that is somewhat less heralded is the Spinal Cerebral Fluid, which is always, even now, coursing through our bodies as our skulls pulse and move at various sutures. Many believe that this fluid to be the seat of the life force.

Each bone in our body holds symbolic and often spiritual significance. The sphenoid, in the center of our skulls, is said to be the cornerstone of our bodies. The Kundalini lies coiled in the sacrum before it rises up through the chakras. The hyoid bone in the throat loves to dance. Each bone moves in a subtle rhythm to support our life force flow. Our ribs pulse and move with each breath, like undulating sea anemones. No bones are fixed.

The Cranio Sacral Rhythm is an almost imperceptible pulse that washes over our entire body. It is distinct from the heartbeat or the breath. It flows and returns approximately once every 3 seconds. By tuning into our own subtle rhythm, we harmonize with nature and reach a place of deep stillness and healing.

In between the body's natural tides ebbing and flowing, needs and emotions are constantly arising within us. It is, essentially, the human condition.

As soon as we begin to accumulate past material (usually as children or even infants), we begin to lose touch with this flow state. We lose the ability to tune into our emotions, because our fields become congested with past emotions, conscious or unconscious. When we are in a state of rigidity, physical and emotional trauma is more easily stored in the tissues. The irony is that when we try not to feel pain, our body stores each of those experiences as tension or dis-ease, and we begin to lose our capacity to feel pleasure.

Hydration is everything. Water is the universal conduit. As we saturate our cells with water, not only does our body evolve, but also our consciousness. Water crystals change their shape based on thought vibrations, as expressed in language and music, as shown by the fascinating research of Masaru Emoto. I cannot think of more powerful evidence for the power of thought vibration as a pure creative force. Thoughts can determine whether a water crystal flowers into a beautiful, symmetrical form, or decays into chaos.

And since our bodies are mostly water, it stands to reason that our entire being is effected by thought vibrations in each moment; those of our own creation and the creation of those around us. Imagine that every water molecule within you is gleaming like a beautiful, crystalline snowflake, delighting at existence. Imagine how this would manifest as our body; how our eyes and our skin would shine!

Apart from being shaped by thought itself, water also sustains the body's systems, which includes facilitating elimination and the natural detoxification process. When we clear toxins from our emotional field, we clear them from our bodies. Conversely, when we shed physical toxins, it clears toxic emotional energy as well. This is why emotional releases are so common during cleanses and fasts. The unconscious does not always know the difference between metaphors and reality, or between the physical and mental realms. Indeed, even consciously we only separate them for convenience.

Tap water is a damaged substance masquerading as water. It's been tampered with. We may be able to clear it with thought, prayer, or blessings, but the odds are against us unless we are already powerful shamans or saints. Fluoride has been known to calcify the pineal gland, at the third eye, inhibiting intuition. So while certain liquid mediums retain the name "water," they do not possess the power to enhance our joyous fluidity.
Chlorine was first used in 1915 during World War I as a chemical agent of death. Now that we have found more

humane ways to kill each other (!), we add trace amounts of it to our water to kill bacteria, but even trace amounts can wipe out our intestinal flora: one of the critical health components of the human system.

In addition, even if we are careful to avoid consuming tap water (which I hesitate to call "water"), studies have shown that showering in tap water is the equivalent of drinking up to eight glasses per day because it absorbs through our beautiful skin. There are a variety of water filters available to mitigate these effects.

We thrive in our fluid state, and if maintaining this state becomes a high priority, the world will continue to evolve.

Kinesiology, or muscle testing, also provides powerful evidence of the power of thought to effect our health and consciousness. Surrounding someone with negative thoughts produces weaker muscle tests in general. As if we need evidence! The "evidence" simply helps us remember the ancient knowledge that we all possessed not so long ago. Perhaps these negative thoughts effect us by altering the molecular structure of our waters.

Being kind to our own bodies is a key to healing, and being around other people who put off positive vibrations produces "miracles" of healing, because it can counteract any negative vibrations we come into contact with, including electro magnetic frequencies, which halt the life force wherever they touch. Our auras protect us when we need protection from forces seen and unseen. It is up to us to keep our own shields fortified.

Foods also put out certain frequencies, and are also effected by thought. I suggest eating mostly water rich foods (at least 80%), and blessing the foods before ingesting. Can you see how this might be beneficial, if food, true food, like our bodies, is mostly water?

Hydration is important, however many of us drink vast quantities of water to compensate for the drying foods we consume (animal products, grains, processed foods, etc). A lot of this water goes toward flushing acid wastes out of the system. A more ideal source of fluids is food. Fluid in water rich foods, such as fruits and vegetables, are naturally balanced with electrolytes and easily assimilated by the body. Monkeys in nature have been shown to drink very little water, as they get most of their liquids from fruits and leaves. Of course, they are vegan, live mostly on leaves and fruits, and eat no grains.

Ayurveda and ancient Chinese Medicine advise against consuming too many raw foods, but I have seen some very radiant, conscious, and healthy people who ate nothing but raw foods or fruits, so I suspect that ancient teachings have been tampered with, or mistranslated over time, either to keep people more grounded or less conscious. Either way, we can experiment with our own bodies and see what works for us. Instead of drinking a sports drink after an aerobic workout, which is loaded with synthetic colors and refined sugars, try eating a melon.

Everything is a network of infinity doubling back on itself countless times. When we become fluid in our body, our mind loosens its grip and we open to higher guidance.

Ideally, we move with the flow of life, as though we are a blossom floating downstream toward all that we desire. Sometimes we get "stuck" for a while until we free ourselves and allow flow again. Being stuck is not necessarily physical, mental, or emotional, though it can be. Being stuck can also be karmic, beyond our comprehension or understanding. Karma can be integrated into our flow and cleared by acceptance. It doesn't matter why we are stuck. It just matters that we move into flow again so that the universe can deliver our highest good. And we will. It is inevitable. The question is, when?

A seemingly subtle shift in thought or perception is all that is needed to move us sometimes. Less often, action is required, if our perception is that action creates change. It really doesn't. Thought vibrations and intentions create our reality, and the same forces re-create our reality time and time again.

Training Suggestions:

1. Morning Super Hydration Practice

Super hydrating is literally retraining the cells to retain more water, and retraining the mind to be more present. I recommend drinking a liter or two of warm organic lemon water upon arising, before the first meal of the day. Aside from hydrating, this practice assists the body in alkalizing, flushes out wastes, aids in elimination, and recharges the chakras. If you don't like lemon, sprinkle a dash of sea salt in each liter. This will help balance out the electrolytes and supply vital minerals so that the body can maintain the hydration levels.

While I believe that the most valuable source of water is the food we consume, this practice starts to bring our hydration levels up quickly.

You may notice skin irritation, cold or flu symptoms, phlegm in the lungs, mucus or yeast in the stools. This is to be expected as water and particularly hot water has a detoxifying effect.

2. Homemade Sacred Water

Since thought forms effect our water so immensely, we can choose to harness this power to transform our lives.

One practice is to write a positive thought on your bottle: something that you desire to resonate more with. My bottle currently says "wisdom" and my friend's says "passion." If you can write this in an ancient language, the signal may be amplified.

We can also speak a positive intention and blow a breath across the surface of our water. This is an ancient Tibetan tactic. We infuse our breath with meaning and we infuse our water with our breath. This works for food as well.

Example:
"I now create a life of ease and flow."

Recommended reading:

The Secret Life of Water by Masaru Emoto

A River of Energy Runs Through Us

• • •

"You must let the psyche move through the meridians. Whether you are tired or not, whether you have energy or you do not, whether you are sick or healthy - these things are like the rain and the clouds, hot weather and cold, winter, fall - a part of life. But if you let your own energy flow through you, you will be all right." - Yogi Bhajan

The meridians make up an intangible, invisible network of energy that courses through the body, like rivers of life force. They run mostly up and down the torso and out into the limbs, connecting various organs and systems. It could take a lifetime of study to truly understand and master this complex network of our anatomy! Some healers can see energy visually. Others "listen" for it or "feel" it.

The beauty is; we don't have to be an expert on esoteric anatomy to flow with the beauty of perfect vitality! Indeed some of the healthiest people have no idea of how these things work! They just intuitively flow in alignment with it.

Stretching can get stuck energy moving. There are specific stretches that effect specific meridians, but you can also do general stretches, or take up Yoga, or try a session of Vibrational Healing Massage Therapy, Thai Massage, Shiatsu, Assisted Stretching, etc. A combination of stretching and deep breathing can produce powerful results.

The movement of energy through the body can be broken down in minute and complex ways. Different traditions also use different terms and symbols for balance and imbalance. But *the blockage of energy is essentially a movement away from our true nature* (through lifestyle, negative thinking, sedentary habits, etc), and *moving back toward our true nature allows it to flow freely again.*

Metal objects can cause energy to coagulate or stagnate. Since energy flows in from the left side of the body and out through the right, wearing jewelry on the left wrist can block energy entering our bodies. In addition, necklaces and earrings can have unpredictable effects on our energy. Wire bras block energy to the breast and cause stagnation of lymph. Stagnation of energy can manifest as breast cancer and other dis-ease, so I suggest finding a suitable replacement for wire bras.

When we enjoy ourselves, cultivate a rich inner landscape, lovingly care for our bodies, nourish our minds, the energy within will flow where it is needed, and leave a trail of bliss and perfect healing in its wake.

Imagination is not Distinct from Reality

• • •

We've been conditioned to think that massive, directed action is the key to manifestation. We've toiled away by night and day, wondering at our lack of fulfillment. But a new distinction is emerging.

Imagination, a right brain function, is the key to manifestation. If we can vividly imagine something, and thrill at the feeling of already possessing it, we can manifest anything. This was what Napoleon Hill figured out when he interviewed the wealthiest men in American in the 1930's.

Health visualizations are a perfect example. Through visualizations, miraculous healings have occurred. Even the densest tumor cannot withstand imagining it moving out of our body, if we cultivate enough faith. And I am not saying it is easy, but perhaps it is easier than I am willing to say, and that is my own lack of faith.

There are layers upon layer of being, and we are connected through karma, past life relations, emotions, and a myriad of other threads that bind us. If we kill a single fruit fly, something dramatic happens in a distant time and space. As we become aware of this, life transforms.

We can only process a fraction of the data that enters our senses and only 10% of what we are is a product of our conscious mind.

In other words, to thrive is to surrender to the mysteries of the universe. To seek to understand what is beyond human comprehension is suffering. This is the great understanding.

Remembering how intertwined everything is; this is one gateway to enlightenment.

What lies wrapped up in the fruit of the farmer?
- o   the soil and all of the creatures that decomposed to fertilize it
- o   the mammal who's manure fertilized it and all of the plants she consumed
- o   the farmer's children that were born while he was being supported by selling the fruit
- o   a myriad of other confluences

In a single orange, an entire universe. We are no different.
Genetically modifying the orange, showering it with pesticides; these things break the chain of connection, shatter the life force, and poison our reality. We are immune to poisons if we choose to be. However, assenting to the destruction of our planet we are not immune to. It wears out our energy bodies, destroys the Earth, and tears at our hearts.

The fact that this reality has been slipping away from us has stripped us of a power we have that is very ancient; our divine birthright. There is no need for anger here. Just awareness. Awareness often leads to awakening. Awareness changes who we are, and as we change, our world shifts and transforms around us.

Language is the creative power. Actually, at a more primal level, sound is the creative power, and language is one way we direct and manifest sound.

"In the beginning was the Word, & the Word was with God, and the Word was God." - John 1:1

Cymatics is fascinating because it shows that certain sounds are composed of a particular vibration that produces a shape when sand vibrates on a metal disk. The nature and frequency of the sound determines how beautiful and symmetrical the image is. Many Sanskrit characters have been shown to produce vibrations whose shape matches that of the written character, which I find fascinating.

We create and destroy through our words. Because we have been stripped of this knowledge over time, we have been shorn of our ancient creative abilities. The power of prayer is the power of words, however, many of us pray to concepts and entities that aren't necessarily empowering.

The source energy, or god, is the only power to make requests to. That force is already within us. Actually we are that force manifest. When we worship the god source within we hold the key to all creation. Making a request to any other being gives them power over us.

Early Buddhists were mortified that people started to worship Buddha as a deity when all he ever asked people to do was look within.

Out of frustration, one master cried: "If you see the Buddha, kill the Buddha." In a non-violent religion, it shows how little they value idolatry.

Words Create, Words Destroy

• • •

"The tongue, like a sharp knife, kills without drawing blood."
- Buddha

Pardon me if I digress. I have a particular soft spot for words.

Words are pure creative power. Over the years, we have been lead astray. And what has lead us astray? Words. Now some of us are skeptical, mistrustful of the power of words, because of the people that have used words to manipulate and destroy. Words are the signposts of thought; revelatory meanderings of the mind and soul.

Words have toppled empires, cultivated heroes, built governments, incited riots, and expressed epic love.

Sound is the first creative principle, and everything arises from sound. Sound is pure vibration and vibration is what we are all composed of. Words are vibration directed. The collective consciousness has embedded certain vibrations with meaning over centuries. We harness this momentous energy when we use words. Words expressed in an ancient language are even more deeply resonant with the fabric of the universe. Sanskrit, Chinese, Latin, etc. The longer a language survives, the more powerful it becomes.

Ancient languages have been infused into the grain of our consciousness. Learning an ancient language empowers us to bless and heal even more effectively, though it isn't necessary by any means.

Caveat: The creative power of words is a double-edged sword. What we focus on enough becomes true for us. The more we write about things we want or don't want, even if the writing is fiction or fantasy, the more we will attract those things into our lives.

As a novelist and songwriter, I have personally attracted many things into my life that perfectly align with songs and novels I've written. Many of these things I do not necessarily want in my life! These days I am far more deliberate while choosing my words.

Language also has a powerful connection to our health or our lack of it. For instance, if we constantly refer to our knees or our back as "bad", we continually anchor that into our body. We amputate that part of ourselves, energetically; our cells go to work diligently to make sure they are in alignment with our thoughts.

Since our mind is constantly creating stories and giving meaning to everything we come into contact with, our body becomes the tangible protagonist of our own story. How do we see ourselves? Are we the center of our story? The righteous hero? The fearless adventurer? Standard bearer of integrity? Or are we sulking on the sidelines, lurking in the shadows, reveling in the achievements or failures of others? Our lives become what is true for us.

Many of us are desperate for a cure; for a healing. In order to seek a cure, we often have to seek a dis-ease. For instance, when we research a dis-ease and we see a list of ailments on a page, some of them may resonate with us. Once we think we have that dis-ease, the body and mind will often manifest more of the symptoms on the list in order to come into alignment with the "label" we've decided to give ourselves. It is similar to going to a doctor for regular checkups. What are we looking for, and if we look for something long enough, don't we usually find it? When something feels "wrong" with our physical body, we sometimes shop around for an affliction, something to blame, instead of looking within.

I always cringe at labeling a disease. Our body is simply sending us a message. It is up to each of us to discover what that message is, and to come back into alignment with ourselves. If we get a rash from time to time, or a stomach ache, or a cough, we might consider speaking: my Alignment Signal is going off; instead of "I have eczema, an ulcer, or bronchitis." Can you feel the difference? When we say I have Celiac's disease, or I have arthritis, or I have cancer, those become a part of our identity. Though we are uncomfortable with our symptoms, sometimes we are happy to have discovered something that makes us uniquely our own. And when we finally do decide upon the label for our dis-ease, we are relieved that other people "have" the condition too, because it can meet our needs for community and connection. The story is that we no longer suffer alone.

The point is, we create our world and our bodies through language. There is no such thing as creativity that is distinct from reality. The relationship between these two is mystical and difficult to trace, but they overlap in profound ways. This is why creative visualizations can harness the energy to heal bodies and minds.

As we become aware of what labels we have attached to ourselves in the past, we can begin to shed those labels like a snake sheds skin, and adopt more empowering ones.

I am so grateful for the messages my body is sending me. I look forward to listening closely and learning from its ancient wisdom.

Emotions as the Key to Happiness and Fulfillment

• • •

Growing up, many of us learned to trust our thoughts at the expense of our emotions. Our thoughts are rational and predictable, whereas emotions seem to arise at the most inopportune times and wreak havoc. They throw us into situations where we seem to have no control.

Over the years, I've joyfully revised this paradigm for myself; thoughts give rise to emotions, and emotions are our guidance system. Emotions that arise are either negative or positive; they either feel good or they feel bad. Good feeling emotions are how we can tell whether we are in alignment with ourselves and with the universe.

Present moment awareness is essential because it allows us to be aware of our feelings so that we may change course as needed. Being in our minds, wrapped up in intellectual pursuits, takes us out of our bodies, where emotions seem to reside in the unconscious. It is not that the intellect is bad, it is just that relying on it at the expense of our emotional faculties is dangerous and counter productive. It is too wrapped up in ego. Even as it tries to create, it destroys, because it seeks to possess and overcome.

The heart-centered energy is different. It allows us to overcome even ourselves, and absolutely dissolve any other obstacles that might lie before us. The heart-centered energy is green. When we desire to connect with the heart, we can breathe and imagine green light flooding into the heart.

Cleansing and fasting can clear "plaque" off of the heart, which also opens the heart chakra. Years ago I read of this in *The Fasting Path* by Stephen Harrod Buhner with some skepticism. It was stated nonchalantly amidst references to Native American mysticism. The skepticism vanished when I experienced the phenomenon first hand on day seven of a ten-day water fast in 2006. I was standing on a street corner in San Francisco, struggling to carry a heavy film projector, when my heart exploded open. I felt intimately connected with all of the anonymous pedestrians swarming around me. I realized that I depended on them as much as they depended on me. We were all a network of energy and matter linked by the threads of community and the chains of love. I stood there in a daze for what seemed like an eternity. The heavy projector lightened in my arms and a tear rolled down my cheek. I started walking again. So this is what it feels like to be alive, I thought. This was and remains one of the pivotal experiences of my life so far.

I often say that I've traveled all over the world, and the greatest adventure of my life happened in my tiny studio apartment in San Francisco during a water fast. In a world where "you get what you pay for," the best gift I ever gave myself was free.

Sweep the Mind with Breath

● ● ●

"A human being is only breath and shadow." -Sophocles

Breath is the essence of life. When we inhale, we take in the life force that sustains us, oxygen, and as we exhale, we release the past, emotional baggage, stress, carbon dioxide, and anything that no longer serves us. A human being can live for months without food, perhaps weeks without water, but only minutes without air.

For centuries enlightened cultures have used breathing practices for healing and spirituality. Saturating the cells with the life force seems to awaken an ancient magic. We become healers and clairvoyants through breath alone.

Being aware of our own breath is a powerful practice.

Breathing into the belly activates the chakras in the core, particularly the heart. It activates subtle Kundalini spiritual forces so that they can move through the body via subtle channels that the ancient Indians called "Nadis." Abdominal breathing is part of many ancient spiritual traditions and can become the core of our life practice.

Whereas high chest breathing takes us into our heads, abdominal breathing relocates our awareness back down into our body. Through this arch we are able to enter the sacred cathedral of heart-centered awareness.

Watch a baby breathe. They breathe so effortlessly into their abdomen. We are born with this gift as we grow we give it away unconsciously.

Training Suggestion:

1. Abdominal Breathing

When we notice ourselves coming into our heads, assailed by a flurry of thoughts, we can breathe deep into our abdomen. With each inhalation, allow the belly to expand, and with each exhalation, allow it to flatten. Breathe in through the nose, and exhale through the mouth. Drop the jaw and allow the air to just move. Try to have the inhalation last as long as the exhalation.

Imagine tension leaving the body as a color that you're not fond of. Inhale peace and healing. Exhale anything that no longer serves. On each exhalation, we can create a subtle sound. This vibration allows trapped energy to move through the throat chakra out into the universe to be recycled.

Do this a few times per day at first. It creates a surplus of vital life force, or Chi, for the body to keep in reserves.

Eventually, as we train our bodies, we will be able to breathe consciously all day long, with each and every breath. Life will transform. Nothing can remain hidden from us when we breathe. The moment opens up to us like a ripe fruit. While we are truly, deeply breathing, we are fully alive.

Fixing the Unbroken

• • •

We are all perfect, whole, and complete in this moment. Radical, eh? Anything out of balance simply means that energy needs to be shuffled around, or nudged from one side of a vast equation to the other. Healing another is essentially healing the self. As we work on ourselves, the other heals. Through history, sages have demonstrated this time and time again.

In the ancient Hawaiian healing practice of Ho'oponopono, one says to oneself (or to Source energy) "I love you, I'm sorry, Please Forgive Me, Thank you" over and over until the person we are "working on" is healed. The person we are working on is always ourselves, as everyone around us is a projection of ourselves. Anything that ails them, ails us.

We are responsible for anything that shows up in our experience. Whatever it is, tumultuous or serene, we summoned it because we needed to experience it for some reason. Unconsciously we felt we deserved it, or we needed it as a stepping stone to learn a lesson, or we felt we needed the comfort of an old pattern.

Once we understand the intricate network that makes up our reality, our time matrix, our harmonic universe, this point becomes paramount. Perhaps some elements will always lie beyond our comprehension, and can only be alluded to in parables. It is not our place in this life to understand but to experience.

Folded into every nuanced point in space time there are alternate dimensions, all possible pasts and futures, ready to explode into our mass consciousness, or unfold mystically like a rose.

As we are healed in this present moment, that healing ripples out into all past and future moments. Our ancestors and our progeny are healed. Even the wildflowers in the meadow or the weeds crawling over the sidewalk feel the healing. We can throw energy out of a body into a plant and the plant absorbs it. If it is too much for the organism to dissipate, the plant will die.

The question then becomes "how do we heal one aspect of reality without injuring another?"

At the cellular level, and in past lives, we've all been recycled so many times that we've become irrevocably entangled into each others' narrative. What if our lover has also been our parent, our sibling, or our worst enemy? As we learn to treat everyone as though they were a beloved family member, we can act out of a love that reflects a more accurate picture of the equation.

The Chakras: How we Plug into the Matrix

• • •

We interface with our reality primarily through our chakras; whirling energy vortexes that run along the spine and light us up like rainbows visible from heaven. (*Please see Figure 1*)

In the ancient Kundalini system, there are 7 main chakras that run up the core of the body, and minor chakras on the hands and feet through which we can heal and share energy with the Earth and one another. Each chakra is connected to life lessons and the organs and tissues in the proximity of it. When our chakras are open, this spin clockwise like miniature tornadoes of light. When they are closed or inactive, they spin slowly, erratically, or not at all. When a chakra is closed, our world feels it.

For example: Many people have issues with Muladhara; the 1st or "root" chakra, located at the base of the tail bone. Issues with physical security and fear effect and are effected by this chakra. When we are not in contact with our root chakra, our posture declares it. We appear unstable physically. The knees turn inward, the feet roll in or out, and often we stand akimbo on one foot instead of both. We are un-centered, off balance, out of touch. The muscles in the legs and feet tend to be lifeless and weak. Often we are not aware of our feet at all. They are not being nourished with vital life essence. As we come into our feet and re-engage our lower halves, our root chakra begins to pulse and oscillate again. We begin to feel safer and more secure.

Some of us can feel the chakras as distinct physical sensations in our bodies; some can see them with their physical eyes, others with their inner eyes, others with their hearts; some listen for the unique frequency they emit; and some just have faith that they are there. The more scientifically inclined can also detect them through measuring electromagnetic resonance.

I don't want to go into excruciating detail here, as there are many beautiful books on the chakra system that draw on a wealth of experience and hundreds of years of study. Each chakra is associated with an element, a seed sound, a color, a form. Specific chakras are replenished by certain foods, sounds, and understandings. Figure 1 is a start, and a reminder for those already advanced in this knowledge.

Because our chakras have more to do with our health than our physical organs, the more energy we give to them, the more time we devote to dancing with them experientially, the more empowered we become to consciously create our lives and live out our destinies.

Recommended Reading:

The Subtle Body: An Encyclopedia of Your Energetic Anatomy by Cyndi Dale
Anatomy of the Spirit by Caroline Myss
Chakras: Energy Centers of Transformation by Harish Johari
Shaman, Healer, Sage by Alberto Villoldo

Love & Gratitude: Our Highest Vibration

• • •

As demonstrated by the stunning research work of Masaru Emoto, water crystals form most beautifully when connected to transmissions of love and gratitude. Thoughts of love and gratitude are the highest, most powerful thoughts we can choose to think. Thoughts give rise to feelings, and as we begin to consciously choose more empowering thoughts, we also retrain our nervous systems and bodies to feel more positive emotions. This upgrades our frequency, which attracts even more positive elements into our lives. Life becomes a fluid dance again, passionately shared with each liquid moment.

Training Suggestion:

1. Gratitude Journaling

The most decisive way to begin to alter our vibration to a state of gratitude is by starting a Gratitude Journal. Before falling to sleep each night, simply write down 3-5 things that happened that day that you could be grateful for if you wanted to. As you write, feel the gratitude swell within you. Allow yourself to smile and allow faces to rise up in your consciousness and smile back.

For those of us that have been out of touch with this reality, starting this process can be tedious. Life seems like a desolate place. But as we get started, the act of looking for sources of gratitude begins to soak into our consciousness. Since we drift to sleep gratefully, we rest better, and our unconscious gets a clean slate from which to process through the night. We cleanse our palate before we enter the dreamscape, as it were.

When I began my own gratitude journal, it was like pulling teeth. So I started simply. I am grateful for the birdsong coming from outside of my window. I am grateful for the clear blue sky. I am grateful for her, him, them. Etc. It doesn't matter where we begin, as long as we begin. The process will soon take over I assure you. Before long, our unconscious mind will constantly be looking for reasons to be grateful, and so, reasons to be grateful will become abundant in our lives.

First, Love Thyself

...

Before we can truly love another, we must begin to love
ourselves again. Almost everyone has critical thoughts of the
self to some degree. Though they are often deeply buried, they
still trickle out in every aspect of our lives. If we are not
careful, we will attract things into our lives that "punish" us, as
we unconsciously feel we deserve to be punished. This is how
I learned to interpret my near death experience in San Diego.
These deeply rooted patterns can manifest in the form of
abusive relationships, "accidents" of all kinds, pain, suffering,
etc.

There are no accidents.   We are brilliant multidimensional
organisms in complete control of our destinies. When
something happens, it is an unconscious choice. It is helpful
that when we undergo an accident, we examine our own
thoughts very carefully to ascertain what state we were in at
the time of the accident. As I lied in bed convalescing after
breaking my neck, I spent weeks in introspection. I wrote a
novel, The Flop Eared Gospels, from my bed. It's about a boy
who breaks his neck and wakes up as a stuffed rabbit. It was
an unconscious purge. What I realized was I had been getting
more and more entwined with a woman for the wrong reasons.
By cracking my 5th cervical vertebrae, the universe was
saying "snap out of it!." I got the message on some levels and
not on others. It takes time sometimes. We humans think that
some things "take time," so that becomes our reality.

As we begin to love ourselves, deeply buried beliefs can
surface. Now we are ready to dismantle them, word by word.
How do we do this? It all comes down to self awareness.
When we stop blaming others for our circumstances, we shine
the spotlight back on ourselves. We take our power back. As
we speak what we desire, or what we think, we can turn
inward and notice what thoughts arise. This can be a very tiny,
subversive voice at first. As we train ourselves, it becomes

louder and louder, until, with practice, we leave nowhere for these deep programs to hide. Through breath and awareness, we chase them out of our bodies and our lives.

Training Suggestions:

1. **Mirror Mirror on the Wall:**

   Look in the mirror and study yourself physically. Look over your face and body carefully. Scrutinize yourself. Let the experience flow. If you feel the urge to flinch or shrink away, just notice. Stand tall and unfold your heart. Love yourself. Fully love yourself, as though you were looking at your beloved, the soul counterpart of your dreams. In fact, there is no one who has stood beside you through so much, with such dedication, shared so much with you. You were there at your birth, your first kiss, and your first heart break. Look into your eyes, into your soul. What do you see? Study the shape of your nose, your mouth. Look at your teeth, your neck, your wrinkles, and your "crow's feet."

   Say aloud: "I love you exactly as you are," and notice the response. Notice any resistance. Any resistance is manifesting in your life in some way, whether as a disease or a difficulty. We don't need to solve every riddle of our life. Riddles will perpetually arise. We only need to solve the riddle of loving the self, and the obstacles will dissolve.

   Mirror work, which I learned of through Louise Hay, is one of the simplest, most direct and poignant methods of bringing unconscious programs to the surface. It is a powerful, spiritual practice, and as you do it more and more, it becomes more and more comfortable. At first it might bring up tears or anger. Continue with it and it will reap untold rewards in every area of your life.

I say something positive to myself, aloud or silently, every time I pass a mirror.

Energetic Amputations

• • •

When we look critically upon a certain part of our body, we unconsciously "deny" that part's existence. We decide not to nourish it. Energetically we lob it off. This energetic amputation can have drastic consequences. It can manifest as pain, any number of dis-eases, or even cancer. Many women often direct critical thoughts at their breasts, and this can lead to breast cancer and other conditions. Men who feel shame and guilt sexually can manifest prostate or sexual problems in their body.

As we remember how to love every part of ourselves, from our ear hair down to our genitals, our bodies begin to thrive. It no longer has to send the pain signal, crying out for love.

Consider what body parts you may have "cut" off in the past.

Are you willing to lovingly accept those parts again, as beautiful as they are?

Training Suggestion:

1. **Self Love Body Scan**

   Close your eyes. Continually speak "I love myself," aloud or silently to yourself. Imagine your body as a vessel and your awareness as a small sphere. As you continually repeat "I love myself" allow the sphere to move through the vessel of your body.

   Notice if there are areas of your body that feel differently than others. Some parts may be open to love and others may be closed. These blockages can eventually manifest as dis-ease in the body, if they haven't already. You may notice the difference visually, as in dark spots versus light spots, as colors, or simply as a feeling. You may notice it in a limb, an organ, or a joint. As you locate blockages, simply keep repeating "I love myself" and notice the area around the blockage soften.

Thank the body and that particular area for sending you whatever message it has been trying to send you. It has been crying out for love, like a frightened, angry child. Celebrate the messenger and the message. It may have saved your life.

Eventually, as the entire body opens to the flood of self love, new possibilities for thriving emerge.

Suggested Reading:

You can Heal your Life by Louise Hay
Your Body Believes Every Word you Say by Barbara Hoberman Levine

Affirmations: Windows to the Unconscious

• • •

Affirmations can be very powerful for retraining the unconscious mind. A popular affirmation is "I love myself." Loving the self is a panacea for almost every ailment. I speak this affirmation to myself many times per day. I use it whenever I notice negative thoughts arising. It is important in moments of survival and growth that we spend as much time as we can sending out positive vibrations. Negative vibrations can attract accidents.

When I used to drive hundreds of miles per day, I knew that me trusting in the universe and in the reliability of my vehicle was critical. Sometimes a flurry of negative thoughts would come flooding into my mind. What if the car breaks down? What if a tire explodes? What would happen to me if my car just died? What if a semi runs me off the road? I couldn't afford to fix the car. The medical bills would be outrageous. I would be out of a job and could never get home. Etc etc.

It is in moments like these, when a quick vibrational shift is needed, that the mantra "I love myself" can work wonders. I use that affirmation as a first-aid measure, and also to test self love physiologically, as in the Mirror practice. I believe that this is why my car never had an issue despite me purchasing it with 127,000 miles on it and adding 100,000 miles over the next four years.

Each week I am usually working on a specific affirmation, based on my goal for that week. I write it across the top of my calendar and read, write, and speak it frequently. Reading, writing, and speaking each ingrain the affirmation into our bodies in a different way. Using them in combination can be very effective.

If we want to test an affirmation, we can speak it aloud and see how it feels. We must be vigilant here. Often the response is very subtle. And as we get the response, we can tweak the language to suit our purpose. We can gauge where a belief is lodged in our tissue, and whether the affirmation takes root.

A few of my favorites:

"I lovingly forgive myself. I am free."
"I now create a world I love to look at."
"I joyously create abundance now."
"I love and approve of myself, exactly as I am."

Louise Hay has created a beautiful list of affirmations, each pertaining to a different body part and thought pattern. I highly recommend her work.

I also recommend studying how the unconscious mind works. There are many beautiful books on Hypnosis, psychology, and Neuro-linguistic Programming that delve deeply into this. Once we understand the power of the unconscious mind, we can learn to use language and imagery to transform our lives.

A good beginning is the book that you are holding in your hand. It is also a good middle, or a good end. I have researched this topic extensively, and tested various techniques both on myself and upon my clients.

Since this book is about healing and thriving, much of what I know about the unconscious has poured out onto these pages, because the unconscious mind is at the root of our patterns. Our unconscious beliefs are, in essence, what decide whether we suffer or thrive.

Fear: Devourer of Love

. . .

"When a man has learned within his heart
what fear and trembling mean,
he is safeguarded against any terror
produced by outside influences."
- The I Ching

I once read somewhere that in Native American belief systems the only natural fears are the fear of falling and the fear of loud noises. All other fears are learned.

When we learn to move through our fear, we transcend the realm of space and time and take on our divine birthright. We have been controlled by our fear; conditioned to react to it. Consider how fear controls the masses. We are taught to "fear" teachers, authority figures, government and religious entities. If we had no "fear", these entities would literally dissolve or evolve.

We are also taught to fear death as a sojourn into a bleak abyss, or the end of everything.
Death is not the end. Death is the beginning. Death is not the concern. Life is. As we master this lifetime, we create a death that empowers us.

A lot of fear concerns arise from Muladhara, or the first chakra, which is located at the base of the tail bone. When we are afraid, we can spread our feet slightly, soften our knees, breathe and get grounded. This will root us in the Earth and make us more aware of our bodily sensations and therefore less susceptible to fear.   We become warriors in the moment.

According to Bruce Lipton's fascinating research, biologically there are only two possible physiological responses in each moment: toward or away from; fear or love. When we live out of fear, love, try as it may, has difficulty entering our life. Passion wanes. Life becomes mundane and stagnant.

When we live out of love, we skirt the edge of danger, push ourselves beyond our comfort zone, and flourish. There is nothing wrong with trembling now and again; it is a sign that we are pulsing with lifeblood and in flow.

When we feel profound fear, our fight or flight mechanism gets activated and our whole being pours itself into our potential response. We evolved this way because our lives were once full of mortal danger. Many of our physiological designs have not yet caught up with our contemporary lifestyle. In any case, whenever our fight or flight response gets activated and we do not get to fight or flee, whatever energy our body has summoned for the fight is stored in our tissues.

Until we release it. On a physical level, the body releases trauma through motion. Trembling can allow trauma to be released with a minimal expense of energy. A lot of fight or flight response trauma is stored in the psoas muscle deep in the hips. A tense psoas can effect Kundalini rising, sexual organs, digestion, and low back pain.

Again, the human animal has much to learn from other animals. Have you ever noticed that after a traumatizing episode, a dog will physically shudder? They don't panic or attempt to suppress it. They allow this natural physiological process to occur; they shake their trauma out. Research has shown that after capturing and tagging an animal, if they are not allowed to go through this process before being released into the wild, they will usually die.

As I was carried away from the ocean on the stretcher, I felt my whole body shivering. I was wearing very little clothing so I thought perhaps I was cold. But it was almost eighty degrees. Sometimes in emergency situations this response is cut short with valium or another muscle relaxer. Fortunately for me it wasn't. I shivered the entire way to the trauma ward, and even while they were attempting to perform the CT scan I was repeatedly asked to be still. I believe that this extended period of trembling greatly reduced the amount of trauma that I stored in my tissues.

The body was designed to be in an almost perpetual state of motion. Motion is flow. Trauma is part of the human experience, but if we can maintain flow even through our fear, trauma gets flushed out before it has a chance to roost. Stored trauma means rigidity and a lack of flow. The fear cripples us. We become congested with it, it becomes entangled in our energetic signature, therefore we attract more to be afraid of.

When we move regularly, our bodily systems can rebalance themselves, and this opens us up to periods of deep stillness. Many of us are caught between movement and stillness. We're frozen in a position at a keyboard, with our fingers pounding away, or we're sitting at a coffee shop, our foot tapping rapidly, unconsciously, our back hunched over a book. Fluid movement contains the whole body. As they say in Tai Chi: "When one part moves, all of the other parts move. When one part is still, the whole body is still."

As I'm working with clients, I often see them resist the urge to twist or flex or writhe. We fear that these spontaneous motions will look strange or that we may not be able to control them. This is societal conditioning and we suffer for it. As I coax them out of their rigidity, and they begin to move again, as they've so desperately longed to move, beautiful things happen. I always smile. It is like watching someone who has been "frozen stiff" break out of a shell.

As we start to move again from the deepest recesses of our instinct, we literally reengage with the moment. We throw off the past like an old, tattered coat and open ourselves to love, to spontaneity, to synchronicity… to flow.

Training Suggestion:

1. Facing Fear Exercise

Take a moment and close your eyes. Take a few deep breaths into your abdomen. Come into the moment.
Now think of something that really scares you. Conjure up an image that is visceral and real in your mind's eye. Don't skimp on detail. Let the fear wash over you.

Gently notice what sensations arise in your body. You may feel it in your heart or solar plexus. It may manifest as a lump in your throat. Instead of shrinking away from it, as you may have done in the past, just be with it. See if you can describe the physical sensation, apart from any "story" about it. Describe the color, the texture, the shape, the sound; whatever comes to you.

Welcome to your fear. This is as bad as it gets. Most of us fear feeling our own fear, more than the fear itself. We run from any semblance of fear. If we run from potential fear, we cannot grow.

As we learn to be with our fear, we see that it is just a sensation, and as we learn to be with our sensations, they pass, as all things do, and new horizons open.

The next time fear arises; you'll know the sensation. Thank it for arising, consider it respectfully, and let it know that you will be proceeding anyway. There are mystical forces protecting each of us and dropping our fear allows them to rise to the occasion.

Ground Zero: Birth Trauma

• • •

The origins of some of our most powerful behavioral patterns can be traced all the way back, beyond our youth, into the womb, where the miraculous, immaculate process of conception begins.

In industrialized nations, where birth is no longer the natural process it perhaps once was, most people are harboring some birth trauma in their tissues. Or perhaps the movement from spirit into flesh is inherently traumatic.

The general consensus is that we are born open, loving, in perfect flow, and we begin to accumulate damage as we move into adolescence. The truth is, many of us have already undergone trauma by the time we are born. This starting point helps to sculpt us so that we may better fulfill our destiny.

Trauma can occur while we are in the womb, or even while we are sperm or egg. Upon first hearing this, I thought that it verged on pessimistic, something like the "original sin" doctrine. But after working with many clients on clearing birth trauma, I now believe that many of us carry some birth trauma wherever we go.

If we choose to work on 1st chakra concerns in this lifetime, chances are we will undergo some degree of birth trauma.
Do you find transitions difficult to navigate?

Birth is our first epic transition. We often pattern our major life transitions after our birth.

Was our birth quick and painless, or slow and agonizing?

Did we refuse to leave the womb, or were we in a hurry to get out and move on? How does this effect who we've become?

Again, there are no accidents. If we suffer birth or embryological trauma, it was part of the life we orchestrated to learn the lessons we chose before we entered into consciousness.

Long before we can process a conscious thought, our cells are busy absorbing information like millions of microscopic sponges. The organism is already planning its survival strategies, and some of these earliest strategies play out as patterns later (much later) in life. Birth trauma can imprint us so profoundly that we may not even notice its effects. It is woven too seamlessly into the fabric of our lives.

Our bodies are brilliantly designed to heal. Sometimes healing just involves bringing new evidence to light. A new awareness can ripple out into all areas of our lives and transform us and those around us.

Consider how delicate a single cell is. If that cell suffers "trauma," all of the cells that replicate after it are already imprinted with that pattern. This is why embryological and birth trauma can effect us so completely.

I have found that in clearing a traumatic pattern, the root of the pattern often reveals itself... the first instance of that pattern. The first point in time and space that the body learned to use that behavior as a "strategy" to survive. Releasing the original pattern undulates through time, to the present, cutting through all of the other instances of "recapitulation" and healing those traumas as well. In my experience, the source of a pattern is sometimes, if not often, birth.
A primary benefit of birth work is that it frees up our lives to unfold unencumbered by the experiences of our birth.

Why Birth Leaves Such a Powerful Imprint

• • •

1. *Birth is a primary foundational experience.* How you were born sets the template for how you will live your life.

2. *Birth Crystallizes karma.* How we are born provides important information about our destiny. When we know our karma, we can begin to renegotiate with and change it.

3. *How we are born effects how we will die.* Clearing birth patterns will allow us to live and die however we choose.

4. *Working with birth promotes spiritual transformation.* Conception and birth are the primary interfaces for psychology and spirituality.

5. *How we are born can effect the process of how we will give birth.* We can recapitulate our birth pattern while giving birth.

6. *Birth is intimately connected to sexual and physical abuse* (there are many similarities about boundaries and types of violation).

7. *Birth is usually experienced within the context of prenatal experiences.* Sometimes the birth is not traumatic per say, but is experienced as such because of prenatal trauma.

8. *Birth organizes all major life transitions.* As our first pivotal transition, it can effect how we behave in all other transitions that follow.

Potentially Traumatizing Events:

o   Unwanted Pregnancy
o   Conception by force, manipulation, or rape
o   Conception under the influence of drugs or alcohol
o   Plans of or thoughts of abortion or adoption
o   Chemical or Emotional Toxicity
o   Emotional, physical, or sexual abuse of mothers and fathers during pregnancy or birth
o   Pre- or parinatal twin loss (1995 research by Keith indicates that up to 70% of pregnancies begin with multiple conceptions but end in singleton births, meaning that twin deaths occur sometime during gestation, usually early on)
o   Accident, injury, illness, or surgery to prenates, babies, or parents
o   Financial Stress
o   Reluctant parenthood (financially or emotionally unprepared)
o   Divorce of Separation
o   Near Death Experience of Parent or Baby
o   Obstetrical Medication and Intervention
o   Birth complications
o   Prematurity (and the medical procedures it entails)

Adapted from the teachings of William Emerson, Ph.D. and Patricia Cramer.

An Immaculate Concept - My Birth

• • •

During my own birth work, I have been fortunate to have made a few connections that shook my hologram.

During my life I have repeatedly attracted hard impacts to my right temple. I have suffered a few concussions in this way, and various less serious incidents. I realized during a birth re-enactment that when the water broke, the right side of my head must have come hurtling down into my mother's pelvis. This trauma kept re-iterating itself over and over because it was such a fundamental pattern.

As soon as I noticed it, I stopped "accidently" knocking my right temple against unforgiving surfaces.

In addition, the part of us that touches our mother's pelvis during the birth process can become "like" the mother. Our cells become like hers in order to avoid the pain. This is one of the earliest strategies available to us, in a watery world where we are forced to endure what comes. We merge with the source of the pain.

This can manifest in fascinating ways, even connecting the behavioral traits of our mother to the body parts that contacted bone on bone. For instance, at certain points in her life, my mother had adopted a victim story. My way of connecting with was through that story. Lying in the hospital bed with a concussion was me playing the victim card. Once I cleared the pattern, I was free to connect with her in healthier and more empowering ways.

When I was born, a cousin of mine, Nicolas, was born at approximately the same time in the same hospital. While my birth was relatively free of complications, my cousin was not so fortunate. He was born with a series of birth conditions that required a host of surgeries. He was born teetering on the edge of this world, between living and dying.

I was welcomed into a world of ambiguity. We were torn that day between celebrating my birth and mourning the tribulations of my cousin. This story surfaced while I was asking my mother about my birth.

More trickled out while I was receiving a regression bodywork session from a master practitioner.

"Are you sure you are ready to go this deep?" she asked. "Things could come up that you might not want to see."

"Maybe in past lifetimes I was afraid to know," I said. "In this one, I'm going all the way. Bring it on."

As soon as I said that, I wondered what I had committed to. We delved in, sparks of energy flew, the silent tears flowed, my soul quivered, and my body shuddered.

On one level, I had always been afraid to shine, dulling my glow, undermining my successes and talents. I did this out of a feeling of guilt that if I shined too brightly, it would cast a shadow on another.

When I made the connection of that pattern to my birth and my cousin, it resonated. My whole body radiated with intense heat and sweat poured off. That's how I knew I was onto something.

My cousin Nicholas committed suicide a few years ago. Somehow an energetic tie was severed that I felt distinctly. May you rest in peace my friend.

These days, I am no longer afraid to shine. And when I feel the urge to dull my glow, I venture within and ask why.

Training Suggestion:

1. **Birth Research- Rediscover your Roots**

   Ask a parent, a grandparent, an aunt, a sibling, or anyone who may know details regarding your birth.

   Notice how you feel as the story unfolds. Notice what resonates with you.

   If there seems to be scant detail, keep probing. There is always more to uncover.

   A few suggested questions:

   o How long was the labor?
   o Was I a planned birth?
   o Describe the emotional environment I was conceived in?
   o What about the physical environment?
   o Was I a Cesarean or a natural birth?
   o Was an epidural used or other drugs?
   o Were forceps used during my delivery?
   o Was I premature or did I come late?

   This can be an intense inquiry for some, depending upon the amount of trauma that was endured. Just listen and be aware, and remember that we each chose our circumstances and everyone is doing the best they can with the resources that they have available to them at the time. Notice the urge to fidget or squirm. Notice any physical sensations.

Cells: Welcome to the Hologram

•••

We live in a holographic universe. Encoded in each microscopic particle of matter or anti-matter, lies the information needed for the recreating the whole universe.

We are wired to thrive. It takes a great deal of conditioning to lock us into the patterns of suffering many of us experience constantly.

Every cell in our body is saturated with memory. Palpating certain cells can cause certain memories to bubble up into consciousness. A vision may arise, or a fleeting glimpse of a brother, a sister, a past life, etc. With the memory, tears may come, a flooding revelation, or the faintest shiver, a subtle vibration, or a wide yawn.

As we release these blockages, we are returning to the flow of source energy. Our vibration begins to oscillate at its designated frequency again, unsullied by past trauma. We are clear to link up with the cosmos in an epic dance.

As we speak about our past, we can choose to be vigilant about the language we use. Just as Freud listened for slips, we can listen to gain clues about what patterns we are carrying.

As I tell my story about my previous head injuries, I notice the word "right temple" coming up. Having spent multiple past lives as a monk, perhaps I was "knocking my head against a wall" looking for the "right temple." That thought came flooding in when I made the connection, as an example. Even in this life, I spent much time searching for the religion that suited me. Was I still seeking the "right temple"?

Synchronistic occurrences give us clues. Numbers show up to light our way. Someone calls and offer the solution to a problem we've been struggling with. Everything is sacred and there are no accidents. First, we learn to read the hologram. It is fascinating and delightful, and as we twist and turn within our own psyches, we heal ourselves and those around us. As our awareness opens, we start play in hologram, like children playing on the seashore, uncovering treasures at every turn.

We are Grace, Embodied

...

I never cease to marvel at the epic beauty of the human form. The physical form itself is a work of art, and as we move in closer, through layers and layers of physiology and levels of being, it becomes ever more unfathomably complex and intricately magical. The body is a storehouse of ancient wisdom. It knows how to take care of itself in ways we could never consciously fathom.

Every conceivable dis-ease that manifests in the body first manifests in the mind or the energy body. For instance anger, unexpressed, can manifest as ulcers or liver conditions.

Since thought patterns are at the root of many (if not all) dis-eases, it makes sense to look there for the remedy. Various studies have shown that even cancer can be dissolved by the power of thought.

The contemporary medical establishment is a new experiment looking to address symptoms rather than causes. At less than a century old, it is already failing. Corruption is rampant in the pharmaceutical industry; side effects almost outweigh the benefits, and the issue gets buried instead of resolved, only to surface later in a form more dire.

However, we can be grateful for the well intentioned among the community and their attempt to contribute to humanity. We can let it all go gracefully as it moves into a more holistic approach. Some will join us and others will scoff at us. Either way, life goes on, and we may choose to thrive or suffer.

As we learn to tune into our bodies, and discover the essence of pain · and dis-ease, we discover the source of our own healing. We receive the sacred and mundane messages that our body is delivering to us in each waking moment.

While the medical establishment is relatively new and minimally tested, many holistic and homeopathic remedies are thousands of years old. They have been tested time and time again, across continents, climates, and centuries. I have literally seen a disease transform after a simple (but powerful) shift of awareness. I have heard of or experienced miracles surrounding fasting, mono-diets, aromatherapy, essential oils, and bodywork.

Holding on creates dis-ease and letting go shatters everything we know and creates space for liquid life! The dis-ease, rootless, gets swept away, like a leaf downstream.

If we are holding anger about a person, for instance, that could manifest as tightness in a muscle or joint, or a liver condition, or an ulcer.

A key to healing is using emotional cues in order to find our way back into alignment. Repressing emotional cues causes dis-ease and suffering. If we work a job that is not in alignment with our nature, and we suppress the cues that our body is giving us over the years, we will experience more and more discomfort and dis-ease until we reach a critical juncture. Our bodies keep sending us the message: transform or suffer; come into alignment or die.

Conversely, moving in the direction of alignment means thriving. We thrive and joy washes over us.

Non-Violent Communication

• • •

The constant ebb and flow of emotions is quintessential to the human experience. Since our mind is always circling, circling, emotions arise continually, moment to moment, in connection with corresponding universal needs.

When a need is unmet in a moment, a "negative" emotions arises. When a need is met, a positive emotion arises. For instance, sitting on the beach next to a partner may feel good. We can check in and say "I feel good because I have a need for connection." We could tweak it again slightly and say "I feel grateful because I have a need for companionship." As we connect to the underlying need, and find an expression of it that resonates, the positive emotion expands. Our vibration blooms. We heal.

Most of our work in the beginning, however, involves "negative" emotions surrounding unmet needs. Sometimes just connecting the emotion to the need meets the need. Sometimes an action, understanding, or request is required.

Though human needs are universal, there are a myriad of ways to connect an emotion to a need and everyone carries different associations. What we can do is stay in touch with our own emotions and their underlying needs, which is nothing short of a spiritual practice. Growing up, many of us cultivate a very minimal vocabulary to express our feelings. As that vocabulary expands, the diversity of our life experience is allowed to grow! We empower ourselves, because instead of seeing emotions as arbitrarily "positive" or "negative", we connect them to needs being "met" or "unmet." We are no longer at the "whim" of a mysterious force called our "emotions".

Basic Formula for Practice:

O.F.N.R.
O. Observation *(an observation of what happened, as literally as possible, without judgment).*
F. Feeling
N. Need *(Underlying the feeling)*
R. Request *(Attempt to get the need met)*

An example:

"Last night when you came home at 1am and slammed the door, I felt angry because I have a need for sleep. The next time you come home late, would you consider coming in through the garage door?"

Can you see how this format could create a safe space of non-judgment? Judgment comes across as accusative and retaliation is inevitable. When we take responsibility for our own emotions, a sacred space of empathy opens up and communication blooms.

By contrast:

"Last night you slammed the door and it pissed me off. I know you only think about yourself, but I need to sleep sometimes. Could you try not to be a jerk just for a few days?"

The difference is obvious right?

Assumptions of Non Violent Communication
o   All human beings share the same needs
o   Our world offers sufficient resources for meeting everyone's basic needs
o   All actions are attempts to meet needs
o   Feelings point to needs being met or unmet
o   All human beings have the capacity for compassion
o   Human beings enjoy giving
o   Human beings meet needs through interdependent relationships

o *Human beings change*
o *Choice is internal*
o *The most direct path to peace is through self-connection"*

I spent years reading the writings of Gandhi and attempting to work his teachings into my life. However, I had still often had trouble connecting with others and making requests to get my needs filled. It seemed that whenever I tried, someone got upset.

The shift occurred when I learned that others were not responsible for my happiness or lack of it. No one "makes" us angry or scared. No one can "make" us happy. No one has that much power over us. We choose our response to each situation in each moment. I was free to formulate requests, and others were free to acquiesce or decline. When someone declines a request, they are not rejecting us as a person; they are simply working to meet their own needs in the moment.

This was a revelation.

I distinctly remember the moment that crystallized this awareness for me. I had spent the entire weekend in a class learning these tools and when I arrived home, late, my girlfriend sat up in bed and began to scream at me. Her words were less than cordial, and intensely triggering. She knew me; she knew how to get a response. However, instead of choosing fear, I chose love. Even beneath the torrential flood of accusations, I saw love. I began to see this woman's underlying needs. Perhaps she was hurt, angry, or scared because she had a need for love, connection, or intimacy. Now we can never presume to know a person's needs without asking, but simply knowing that they were there created a massive shift in awareness. Time fell away and that "enlightened" feeling washed over me again. She felt that me working all weekend meant that I loved her less. She wanted me to do something to show her otherwise. When I saw this flash, my whole body softened and my eyes filled with tears. Seeing this vulnerable, lovely creature trying so desperately to connect with me really moved me. I dropped what I was holding and I lied beside her, and we spent the next twelve hours in bed, celebrating one another, and the rest is history.

I can honestly say that this awareness transformed me. Life has unfolded, and the miracle of human connection now surrounds me. I am so grateful. Communication is seen as an open ended stream of feelings and needs, ebbing and flowing. Keeping the dialogue open allows emotions to flow freely without getting stored in the body or exploding in violent outbursts. It's written all over my face: I smile more and when I look into my own eyes in the mirror, I see a new light.

Training Suggestion:

1. **I Feel Because I Need**

   Can you see how relationships based on this level of openness and understanding might be more likely to thrive? Are you open to continually refining the process until your relationships are inspiring and full of joy?

   The simplest place to start is to begin tracking your own feelings and needs.

   There are Non-Violent communication lists which I suggest you use at the beginning, as your emotional vocabulary begins to expand.

   It also helps to learn it by practicing it with others. When we're triggered, we often lose touch with our resources, and another can help us make connections we might not otherwise have made.

   Approach a friend, and ask if there is anything that they are currently dealing with… any emotional issue. Start with something relatively minor. As they tell the story, just listen, openly.

And then begin to explore by asking: "I would like to learn more about what you are going through. Would you mind if I ask you a few questions so that I can better understand?"

And then begin the inquiry.

Are you feeling X because you have a need for Y?

They may correct you and refine your words. This is all part of the process. We are only guessing, but even taking the time to guess shows someone that we care.

When the need is identified, you will know. Something dramatic and distinctly human will happen. Tears or laughter. Welcome it.

And beware because some "feelings" are actually judgments masquerading as feelings. Such as I feel betrayed, or rejected. Stick to the list and encourage them to stick to the list as well.

Recommended Reading:

Non-Violent Communication: a Language of Life by Marshall Rosenburg

Food as Vibration

• • •

Just as our emotional responses effect our vibration, so does the food we ingest. Food is energy. Each morsel has its own electro-magnetic signature. Whole, raw, live foods bring us into balance, our natural state. They hone our intuition and open our hearts. We thrive.

Processed "foods" bring us out of balance. They weigh us down, dull our senses, and cause energetic imbalances and neurological dysfunctions. That is how simple it is. Some of us have never even had "food." We've lived on processed marketing experiments. It is a wonder we are still alive.

How glorious the body is to perpetually rid us of these wastes, day after day, year after year. It is nothing short of a miracle. Another miracle that is so simple it's almost difficult to believe.

There are raw foodists, fruitarians, even breatharians. These beings shatter our paradigms. The point is, food is only a tangible matrix that stores energy. It is the energy itself that sustains us.

As we begin to come back into alignment with our higher selves, the matter side of the equation starts to matter less.

We become less dense, and require less calories.

I have a friend who lived on only 500 calories a day, but they were high quality calories. Wheatgrass, fermented coconut milk, chia seeds, raw and vegan.

Most people are literally weighed down by pounds of unprocessed wastes festering in their colon. The need for an abundance of protein is a myth that has been perpetuated for hundreds of years, for various reasons, each one more absurd than the next. Mostly the myth keeps humanity unenlightened, frightened, broken. Not to mention that we are creating a massive, surging vibration of fear emanating from slaughterhouses.

Have you ever seen how beautiful a deer in the woods is? It almost feels like a kindred spirit, doesn't it? Conversely, have you seen a genetically modified chicken crammed into a cage in inches of its own feces, with broken wings and legs, living a life of slow degradation until it fearfully transitions to death? Would we willingly put this energy into our body?

We have been massively programmed for generations. Programming is rampant and deep and billions of dollars are continuously funneled into it every year. This is in addition to the programs we acquire growing up, which are not quite as insidious but still do damage. We are rewarded with food, for example, or we are given food to comfort us when we are in pain.

Instead of eating for the nutrients, we often eat for other reasons, conscious and unconscious. We eat to entertain ourselves, to reward ourselves, to fill space where we want to experience a sensation.

There are people that put on weight in order to deter members of the opposite sex. Conversely, there are people that put on weight to appear powerful and larger than life. As we bury our ideal selves in layer upon layer of fat, we lose touch with what we are.

Instead of shedding the fat through willpower, we can strike at the seed of the program, hack at the root, begin to love ourselves again, and watch the fat melt off like candle wax.

Mass produced cow's milk is poison. It is pasteurized and saturated with puss, chemicals, and antibiotics. It is infused with the fear and suffering of the creature that offered it. It produces a confluence of mucus in the body which takes time to remove and inhibits nutrient absorption. It floods the blood with acid, which the body has to scramble to neutralize by drawing calcium from the bones.

The milk myth is pervasive. I grew up forced to drink milk, which I never really liked, so that I could grow to have "strong bones." As it turns out, I had an undiagnosed milk allergy. I often had to spend my days as an infant in the hospital having mucus drained from my lungs. I remember the sucking sound and the rubber hoses as I writhed on a cold table covered in paper. Cheese is concentrated milk and salt.

When we notice the urge to partake in milk, which is more of an addictive, emotional need than a physical one, we may consider indulging in raw milk or cheese. Raw goat milk is probably the easiest to assimilate.

However, pretending that milk has health benefits will never serve us. There is more calcium in most green vegetables than there is in milk.

As we shatter the programming, our natural appetites begin to return, and as we live by their guidance, we begin to thrive again.

We Cannot Live on Bread Alone

•••

I gave up gluten in 2002, when I discovered that I had an allergy to it. The sign was a persistent rash on my face along the stomach meridian. I had a blood test for antigens that confirmed this. Eggs, dairy, and green beans also showed up on the test.

Gluten is the protein found in many grains, including wheat, rye, barley, and spelt. Whether sprouted, refined, or whole, the gluten remains in the finished product. Gluten is wreaking havoc on the health systems of the world because our bodies are not adapted to eating these grains as a staple. As agriculture advanced, we began to eat more and more of these grains because it was convenient. In addition, we feed massive quantities of them to the animals we consume, so trace amounts remain in the flesh. Livestock raised on grains produce fattening meat with unnatural omega fatty acid ratios. When this livestock is grass fed, however, these ratios come back into balance and meat becomes food again, though it still creates an abundance of acid in the body, which must be flushed out.

Gluten causes issues with the thyroid and the digestive tract. Most gluten these days has also been genetically modified for ease of growing and pest resistance. This genetically modified product scarcely resembles the original grain on a molecular level. Some gluten is probably tolerable, but many of us eat it at every meal, and often refined versions of it, which means it lacks the fiber to move itself through the digestive tract.

Also, grains take a lot of water to process. Though they are marketed as being fibrous (and they are) vegetables and fruits are fiber with water, and pass through the system easily, generating energy. When I personally eat grains I feel sluggish and dehydrated. I often drink a liter of water soon after consuming grains in order to rehydrate. In addition, consuming grains with proteins inhibits digestion. Protein requires an acidic environment to digest and starch requires an alkaline environment. These are the two most difficult molecules for the body to digest, and this difficulty is compounded when they are taken together.

The higher the water content of a food, the easier it is for the body to assimilate it.

Apart from water content, a food is either acidic or alkaline based on the minerals it contains. Fruits and vegetables are alkaline, and animal products and grains (in general) are acidic. When acidic foods enter our bodies, our bones release minerals into the blood to keep the blood alkaline. As these alkaline reserves run dry, our bones become brittle and we age. Some people postulate that this, as well as dehydration, is why elders shrink physically. In acidic environments, cancer, yeast, tumors, and various dis-eases thrive. In alkaline environments, the body is fully empowered to engage these threats. There are many books and websites discussing the acid / alkaline balance. Since it is absolutely critical, I wanted to at least touch on it here. If we eat mostly water rich foods, we are naturally alkaline. Most people, however, eat mostly acidic foods that also contain very little water. This is a recipe for inevitable disaster, and precipitated my own health crisis on more than one occasion. (Some of us learn slowly).

Some foods create an acidic response in the body, but so do many thoughts, such as anger and resentment. Again, we see that the physical and emotional elements are closely entwined.

I am not generally one to be taken in by conspiracy theories, but it may be the agenda of certain organizations to destroy human health. Some industries profit by this (healthcare), and others simply see it as collateral damage as they rake in our energy in the form of money (fast food conglomerates). If we sense that an entity or an organization is attempting to destroy our health, we can thank them for their time and move on, back into a state of ease and flow. Anger is more empowered than apathy, but love and gratitude are more effective options here.

The ideal foods are whole, raw fruits, vegetables and sprouts, (mostly fruits), raw natural oils, raw nuts and seeds. If we eat nothing but these, we will thrive.

We may need to do some investigating to discover what works for us. Ideally we eat seasonal food based on the climate that we've adapted to. These adaptations probably occurred hundreds of years before we were born. Our blood type can provide clues about our ancestry.

As we eat whole foods, begin to move our bodies aerobically, and cut chemicals out of our diets, we take back our birthright as living, liquid beings that thrive on joy and human connection. The symptoms of detoxification may arise as our body purges a lifetime of toxins. Celebrate this gratefully. The miracle of our human body is coming back into alignment with the loving universe that created it. We are becoming children of the stars again.

Training Suggestion:

1. **Lemonade Matrix Clearing**

   I suggest starting a dietary change with at least a 10 day Master Cleanse, which is a liquid cleanse where only Lemonade made of maple syrup, lemons, and Cayenne pepper is consumed. I prefer this to water fasting for those new to fasting. It is gentler on the system and the consciousness. Detox symptoms aren't as severe and the "healing crisis" can be less intense. After the cleanse, the natural appetites and energies return, if temporarily, and you can use this time to re-calibrate your lifestyle and food choices for optimal thriving.

   Our "gut instinct" can be impaired by a damaged intestine, which is often caused by stagnation of wastes in the colon. Yeast and other bacteria and parasites can bloom out of proportion unchecked. The cleanse helps to reset this mechanism, though it may take a few to get the intestines fully healed again.

Once the intestine is damaged, and many of ours are, starch, particularly refined starch, damages our intestinal lining even further.

2. Blessing Food

(Adapted from American Indian Secrets of Crystal Healing by Luc Bourgault)

We can use our energy to alter the energetic properties of our food as well as our water.

First, taste a small morsel of food. Notice the subtleties of how the food tastes and how the body responds to it.

Rub your hands together for about thirty seconds. This activates the secondary chakras in the palms and balances the hemispheres of the brain to enhance powers of perception.

Now, separate your palms and imagine that you are holding a ball of radiating energy. Feel the warmth and the quality of this energy. Even if you can't feel it, it is there.

After rubbing your palms together, as described above, you can hold one or both over the food you are about to consume. In anywhere from 10 seconds to a few minutes, you should be able to feel a palpable sensation of your hands rising. Your food has been energized.

Now taste again and see if you notice the difference. Vegetables and fruits take a few seconds to energize, whereas less healthy alternatives may take up to four minutes.

In addition, if there is an animal product on our plate, we can speak a prayer for the animal and blow on the food or the bones. This is how Tibetan Buddhists are able to eat meat despite their Buddhist beliefs of non-violence. We use the meat passing into our lives as an opportunity to bless it. Thus we improve the future of the animal.

Example:

"Beloved creature, thank you for nourishing my body this day. May you be reborn into a blissful place of thriving."

Recommended Reading:

The Master Cleanse by Stanley Burroughs
Breaking the Vicious Cycle by Elaine Gottschall
The Heretic's Feast: A History of Vegetarianism by Colin Spencer

Skin – What Connects Us

• • •

Our beloved epidermis is the largest organ we have. It protects our body from the elements and from danger. It allows us to feel out into the word via titillating sensations. It insulates us from the cold and from certain energies. It regulates our temperature so vital organs can continue to function optimally. Without skin, life as we know it would change. Sex, tender passion, physical intimacy would need to be foregone or recreated.

Anything that we apply topically onto our skin absorbs into our body. Lathering on chemical sunscreens and petroleum based products pollutes our bloodstream and taxes our lymphatic system, our kidneys, and our liver. The same goes for soaps and shampoos.

By being aware, we can avoid putting anything on our skin that we wouldn't put into our own mouths.

In addition, washing our face and hair constantly with harsh soaps and hard water removes the vital oils that keep us young and vital. I know of an old woman who claims to never wash her face, and though she is in her eighties, she looks forty. She simply wipes grime off of her face with a washcloth, which also exfoliates gently.

Our skin is designed to self regulate, heal, and glow. When we trust it, it shines.

Death Becomes Us

• • •

When I began working with clients and witnessing them regress into past life experiences regularly, my concept of death began to evolve. I had studied Buddhism thoroughly and the concept of Karma. Though I understand it intellectually, I also understand that there are aspects of it that are beyond comprehension. I have also read many case studies of Near Death Experiences, and the evidence is overwhelming that death is not the end of our consciousness. In my current practice I also work to clear "energetic" attachments from the body, which sometimes manifest as disincarnated spirits clinging to another body out of confusion.

As we begin to understand that our life was constructed so that our soul could learn lessons, and our death is a transition into a new life with new lessons (or a transcendence of the mortal form entirely, once we're "finished" growing), the fear of death loses its grip on us.

As I stated previously, I have experienced brief glimpses of "enlightenment", and I was mowed over with peace. I saw life and death meld together as one seamless unit. My goal is to be able to "guarantee" enlightenment for my clients. Of course, that wreaks of the same audacity I harbored as a child. I think of all of the Zen masters who attempted to transmit their wisdom, their state of being, to so many students without success. Perhaps they didn't have the tools or the technology. Perhaps less people were ready then. Perhaps it is the intrinsic nature of "enlightenment" to be rare by definition. If everyone were enlightened, our language would no longer require the word.

When we are infants we are fluid and "light." During life we accumulate density through traumas and memories. We become denser and more solid.

I have hopes that we can move back toward that incredible lightness of being, live lives of radiance and joy, and ascend at the end easily and naturally.

What would you need to resolve if you knew that you were going to pass away any minute, any day?

Training Suggestions:

1. **Rehearse your Death**

> Lie in a quiet place where you will not be disturbed. Place your hands at your side, and remove all superfluous comforts. You have just died, and you are lying in your coffin. Imagine lying there as family and friends come from miles around to pay their respects. Listen to their speeches. Bear witness to their tears. Are there many or few? What are they saying? Did you leave behind the legacy you expected to leave?

> As we rehearse this scenario, we are actually scripting future events, and stripping away the fear associated with death. Death really is the final frontier, and the great unknown. To presume to be afraid of it assumes too much. Experience everything that you think it might be, and see that it cannot match your fears.

> If we can pass away in serenity, we can navigate the stages of death with grace and equanimity. We carry our poise from life beyond.

2. **Say the Unsaid**

> Create a list of things that you have never said, and a list of people with whom you have unresolved issues. What would it take for you to resolve those now, if not for both of you, at least from your own perspective? Send letters, make phone calls, and bestow gifts.

If you cannot locate the person you have withheld your truth from, have another stand in for them. Speak into the eyes of the other that which you've withheld. Allow them to just be there to witness. Having a witness, any witness, can be a liberating experience. I often have clients speak things to me that they have never spoken to anyone.

Though I am a stranger, the mere act of saying the unsaid with a witness releases it from the body and allows life to flow more freely. If we cannot find a witness, we can witness ourselves.

To die without baggage is to be born without baggage, and there is no reason we can't start shedding extra baggage now, before the end is nigh.

3. Little Deaths

We live in a perpetual cycle of life and death. Each and every second we are alive, it is estimated that up to three million cells die and nearly that many are reborn. People come in and out of our lives. Moments, seasons, days, nights all arise and pass.

We can use these miniature deaths as meditations on the nature of being.

"The only thing constant in life is change." - Francois de la Rochefoucauld

Clearing Trauma: Releasing old Ways of Being

• • •

We express our full potential when we are fully present in each moment. As Louise Hay writes: "The point of power is always in the present moment." Holding onto trauma, consciously, unconsciously, or physiologically, is allowing our energy to be siphoned off into the past. Clearing trauma opens up vast stores of energy for us to use in any way we choose. The effect is often palpable. After trauma is cleared, we feel freer and lighter, more aware of our bodies, and less susceptible to unconscious patterns that run our lives from behind the scenes.

The Physiology of Trauma

• • •

Everything that enters our field is stored in our cellular memory and / or our unconscious mind (is there a difference?). This really illustrates the power and beauty of the mind / body / spirit connection and the pervasive nature of the hologram.

When something enters our experience (we might say "happens to us," though that downplays our own role in our life experience), and it "hurts" us, sometimes the pain is too much to bear in that moment. Intense pain triggers a mechanism so that some pain is felt, while the rest is "stored" away. This is a natural response to pain. An unnatural but still pervasive response is that we consciously numb ourselves with synthetic mood altering substances or experiences in order not to feel.

In any case, the "pain" is stored in our tissues and our unconscious mind, rippling out into our lives constantly, playing out in patterns and the way we interact with everyone around us. Until we bring up the old pain again, and fully "feel" it, we are not fully free of its affects.

Naturally, it trickles out over time, through "leaks" in our language (Freudian slips), dreams, physical pains, behavioral patterns, etc. My work in trauma release and transformational bodywork can open a floodgate that allows it to pour out.
A few questions may be springing to mind about now.

Will too much pain flood out at once, and overwhelm me?

No. The conscious mind has a filter, and it will only allow the release or re-patterning of things we are ready and able to face, physically and mentally.

Will recalling the trauma bring up more trauma?

No. Each time we experience the trauma, the effect on our physiology is lessened. Also, always remember that the re-experience will never be as "intense" as the original or "seed" experience, and you made it through that experience just fine. (Right?)

Are you aware of any events in your life that you know were "stored" in your body?
Here are a few catalysts to jog your memory…

Some potential sources of trauma are:

- **Birth** (I'm not convinced that birth is inherently traumatic, though obstetrical intervention perhaps exacerbates the ordeal)
- **Physical Injury** (as scar tissue is palpated, memories of the scarring event can rise to consciousness)
- **Past Life Injury** (some pain is so intense we carry it across lifetimes)
- **Emotional Injury** (emotional pain is often stored around the heart or in the intestines and hips, though it can literally be stored anywhere in the body)

The Sacred Metamorphosis

•••

As these "unfelt" memories are reintegrated into our awareness, beautiful transformations can occur. It can also leave our energy more emotionally clear, so that we get clearer emotional signals in the future. This is immensely valuable, considering that our emotions are, in many ways, our most accurate "guidance" system.

Transformational Bodywork, Vibrational Healing Bodywork, Cranio Sacral Balancing, Yoga, Transformational Breathwork, Somatic Psychology, etc, can access these memories through the physical body, and Holistic Life Coaching and Transpersonal Hypnosis can access them through the mental body. Spiritual disciplines like meditation Tai Chi, and yoga, can access them through the spiritual body.

Once the memories and / or emotions arise, they can be shifted, scrambled, restructured in a variety of ways. Sometimes the arising itself clears them, which I refer to as "Trauma Release." Sometimes, Trauma Posturing and physically re-enacting the traumatic event can change the associations, which I refer to as "Trauma Repatterning."

As these old patterns begin to clear, there is often a period of integration and increased bodily awareness. Sometimes this means disorientation, tiredness, headaches, and physical aches and pains. It can manifest in many ways, and is usually short lived. The point is to see the pain as valuable feedback, instead of attempting to hide from or suppress it.

Usually, there will be glimpses of "enlightenment" peppered through the experience, and then the old patterns will reassert themselves. It is ideal if a transformation be sustainable and graceful, though that is not always an option. In any case, once we interrupt the pattern, it is imperative that we keep conditioning the new pattern until it sticks.

As we drop the bonds of the past, it opens us up to a realm where possibilities are endless: the present moment. As we access this momentous power, our consciousness evolves and life begins to change for us in a holistic way. For instance: while working on our relationship, we notice that our financial situation changes; while working on our negative self talk, we notice that our career gets an overhaul; while working with our relationship to our parents, our fitness improves.

Are you open to releasing yourself from the past, and opening yourself up to a life of extraordinary possibilities?

Awakening the Light Body

· · ·

We are a network of oscillating energy. Each of our chakras vibrates at a certain frequency, as do each of our organs, glands, and tissues. This combination of frequencies creates our aura. Our aura is a network of geometric energy patterns that surround our body in an egg shape, and can extend from just a few inches to over forty feet, depending on our health and surroundings. Our aura vibrates at a higher frequency out in nature. It blooms out into the space and networks with the surrounding life. We teem with the teeming life around us. In the city, surrounded by other spirits, our auras shrink to cocoon us more closely.

Our auras offer us energetic protection. Nothing at a lower frequency can harm us energetically. When our frequency drops, we can suffer energetic attachments that can drain our energy and effect our personality.

What can weaken an aura:
- o Processed foods
- o A lack of Integrity
- o Chemicals (GMOs, MSG, pesticides, artificial sweeteners, pharmaceuticals)
- o Recreational Drugs and Alcohol
- o Negative Emotions (Our own and others')
- o Sleep Deprivation
- o Exhaustion
- o Unresolved Trauma
- o Dehydration
- o Physical Injury
- o Posture and Positioning
- o Electromagnetic Frequencies
- o Cigarette Smoke
- o Environmental Pollution

Our Bodies Know More than We Do

• • •

Our bodies are sponges. Everything that happens to us is recorded in our energy matrix. Our unconscious mind links up to the super-conscoius mind, which directly interfaces with the source of creation; it knows all. If something brushes us in our sleep, even if we don't have or never had conscious awareness of it, it is recorded in our body/ mind/ spirit complex. Accessing the subconscious mind via hypnosis can reveal an astonishing level of detail regarding memories we didn't even know we had.

Someone can be hypnotized, for instance, into believing that the person standing in front of them doesn't exist. After this state change, they are able to read the clock behind the person standing in front of them. What changes during the hypnosis session? The client's belief system or reality in general? Is there a difference? How can believing that someone doesn't exist allow another to see through them as though they were transparent?

The Life Giving Sun

...

"Ring the bells that still can ring. Forget your perfect offering. There is a crack in everything that's how the light gets in." - Leonard Cohen.

The sun is foundational to our existence and our experience. If the sun did not exist, and we were not in proximity to it ,we would not exist as we do now. A confluence of influences had to line up perfectly in order for human life to evolve and thrive. We are fortunate to exist at this moment, in this epoch.

Over centuries, we have evolved to spend most of our time out in direct sunlight. Synthetic modes of protection (chemical sunscreens, windows, and sunglasses, for instance) alter our bodies' natural ability to utilize ultraviolet rays as nourishment. The chemicals in sunscreen soak into our bloodstream almost instantly and have been linked to cancer and other dis-eases. The prolonged use of sunglasses weakens our vision and impairs the ability of the eyes to adjust to natural light.

The only natural sunscreen that aligns with our grand design is shade. That is, when our skin has had enough sun, we can cover our skin with clothing and hats, or seek shade under a tree or indoors.

The mindset is an important factor in the equation as well. If we consider the sun an insidious force raining destruction and skin cancer down upon us, it will fulfill that vision. If we consider the sun a blessed source of nourishment and energy it will fulfill that vision.

The sun is the most powerful force we know of, other than love. It sustains an entire solar system by merely being. It is fortuitous that we've been placed on the Earth, and circumstances (there are no accidents) allow us to thrive and enjoy the life-giving sun.

Training Suggestion:

1. Here Comes the Sun

o Cease the use of chemical sunscreen and sun block
o Ditch the shades
o Alkalize (When the body is alkaline, minerals are balanced and the skin can function optimally, helping to avoid sun damage)
o Super hydrate
o Ingest natural, raw, organic, life giving oils (flax, coconut, grape seed, olive, etc)
o Rejoice in the sun, and feel its healing properties
o Continually increase time spent outdoors

Relationships and the Meaning of Life

• • •

What are romantic relationships for? Joy? Pleasure? Transformation (sometimes painful)? Magnification of experience? Balancing of sexual energy? Spiritual union of souls? I can safely say that if I knew the answer once, I no longer do. I'm leaning toward "magnification of experience" with some hesitation.

Here's why...

Essentially my partner, a beautiful soul with a "tough" history, who I had lived with for almost two years, met another and became enraptured. She explained to me that though she loved me more than any man, she could not ignore the pounding of her heart, and the ineffable draw toward her soul counterpart. Her counterpart, in this case, was another woman.

There are schools of thought that say that whatever is going on in your relationship, endure, because you are there to bring to the surface and explore all of your issues. Our lovers are just mirrors of ourselves. I tried that, for about a week. While she was out with her new fascination, all night, I lied in bed in anguish, facing my own abandonment issues (we all have some). I looked at her empty half of the bed, and just cleansed my spirit with tears. I resisted watching a movie or listening to music. I resisted distractions, as I often instruct clients to do. It isn't easy, I thought, grinding my teeth, relaxing my jaw. I deliver the idea to clients with ease, but when we're triggered, it's difficult, no matter how evolved we are.

My personal school of thought says that sometimes the universe is bludgeoning us with signs, and ignoring them is not only reckless, but also impossible. She was not my ideal mate, I realized, and I had been trying to convince myself otherwise for years. Something had to arise to force a change.

I am an energy worker, a healer, and a holistic life coach, working to bring my whole life into congruence. How long could this blind spot possibly endure?

A few months after this I was trained in The Work, which was created by Byron Katie. During the training, I found all of the assumptions that I had been entertaining about my lover were illusions that I was holding onto so hard that they were actually choking the life out of me. As I released them, with a trickle of tears, I felt so much love and gratitude for her, and I truly understood her dilemma. Instead of being a childish, selfish, foolish person, I saw her as being brave, confident, mature, and authentic. She was being courageous to explore this other side of herself.

I know that she will forever be a part of my life, if only holding space in my heart. I no longer call her out of neediness, but simply out of love. Usually I just give her the space she seems to need to clarify her desires.

And like magic, coming into alignment with who we are allows our desires to manifest almost effortlessly. As Paulo Coehlo writes in The Alchemist, "When we are moving toward our Personal Legend, the universe conspires to help us achieve it." Similar concepts come across in *Ask and it is Given* by Jerry and Esther Hicks.

With her everything felt like a struggle. Since leaving her, I have manifested many things I had been desiring for a long time. A beautiful guitar, a motorcycle, an inspiring living space, an incomparable roommate, a host of new friends, a network of business connections. I began writing songs again and the music just seemed to flow.

I had also wanted to relocate to the Bay Area from Elk Grove for about a year. When it came down to it, one moment made it inevitable. Since I was authentic in expressing my needs and desires, many generous souls opened their doors and their hearts to me.

Just like a rainbow follows the storm, a breakdown is often (if not always) a breakthrough in disguise.

So while I didn't ask for heart break, I did ask for intensive life training. That seems to be exactly what I got. Next time I'll remember to be very specific about what I ask for.

Thank you universe for delivering me to my highest good. All is well in my world.

The Full Moon, Fasting into Sanity

• • •

For whatever reason, the full moon wreaks havoc on the human system. Studies have shown that violent crimes such as homicide and rape increase under the light of a full moon.

The legendary Chinese poet Li Bai drowned attempting to embrace the reflection of the moon in a pond. I feel for ya, Li Bai. I once attempted to drive across the country (from Phoenix to Chicago) in the middle of the night for what I thought was love, and realized only later that the full moon had had me in her grips. This happened twice, come to think of it, on two non consecutive occasions.

Now, having been tempered a little with the wisdom of age, I know myself well enough to feel moon crazies coming on.

As a monk in the order of Ananda Marga put it, paraphrasing the words of their founder:

"Baba tells us that the gravitational pull of the moon effects the oceans of the earth as well as the liquid portion of our body. On certain lunar days that force creates disturbance in the body and draws the fluids upwards creating undue pressure on the higher chakras, thereby inhibiting the mind. By fasting on the proper day we can offset this negative effect by keeping the stomach empty, in which case a vacuum results and the higher chakras are not adversely affected. For these reasons and more, we should all be vigilant to fast on the proper day..."

Now that I have fasted in the light of many a full moon, I can physically feel the effects of the incipient event as physical sensations in my body, such as a lessening of the appetite and a restless sensation. I start to feel the lure of poetry and Paris for instance, and am easily lured off center, out into the land of ravenous appetites. Fasting and general awareness empower me to remain centered and to witness the gravitational pull and just be with it until it passes. The sensations generally last about 3 days

Training Suggestion:

1. Fast at the Full Moon

In my experience, dry fasting is the most effective one day fast to use on the day of the full moon. Dry fasting means taking no food or water for the day of the fast. Drinking a mixture of warm water mixed with sea salt and lime or lemon in the morning, to flush out the toxins that have accumulated in the colon, can be efficacious. Studies have shown that if activity is kept to a minimum, the body will not become dehydrated despite the dry fast... it will do everything in its power to retain water.

If a dry fast is impossible, or if you'll be under duress or exertion, a water fast is acceptable. And if fasting at all seems difficult or impossible, just being aware of the lure of the moon can have dramatic effects on physiology and behavior.

An affirmation springs to mind:

"I live in a peaceful and loving universe. All is well in my world."

Holistic Vision: Windows to the Soul

• • •

"Without a vision, people perish." Proverbs 29:18

I had vision problems growing up. I was plagued with headaches caused by eyestrain. When I looked up from a book the world was a blur. Vision seemed a downward spiral.

Once, while visiting an eye doctor in the hopes of being prescribed glasses so that I could see, an interesting, serendipitous thing occurred. My doctor was out, and had been replaced by a substitute. This man was kind of radical at the time. "You could get glasses," he said. "But your eyes will start to depend on them and get weaker over time. Or I can show you some exercises you can do to strengthen your eyes." I did the exercises religiously. For a few months. Then stopped entirely.

Years later, I was wearing glasses. I had kind of given up on the exercises. It wasn't that they weren't effective, but just that I hadn't gotten the whole picture. After wearing glasses for some years, I decided to give it another chance. I was an artist after all, and my vision was a part of my livelihood. I read every book on the topic that I could get my hands on, and I began diligently formulating and practicing the tips below. I am happy to say that I no longer require glasses and the world has taken on a vibrancy that I never could have imagined. I believe that this natural vision improvement is available to almost everyone.

First of all, if you're even reading this, I would like to acknowledge you for having the faith in healing and in the beautiful design of your own body. This faith reaps a wealth of rewards.

Only a fraction vision problems have to do with a malfunction of the eye. Since vision is mostly about how the mind uses the eyes, problems are mostly a matter of perception and understanding. Eyes that function are fluid, fluttering, and adaptable to many circumstances.

If we are very open to our experience of our vision moment to moment, we may find that on vacations, or in relaxed settings, our vision becomes clearer. Tension creates an energy blockage and thus impairs vision. Relaxation allows vision to flow.

Our eyes can literally adapt to almost any circumstance. If we begin to rely on prescription glasses or contacts, the eyes adapt by becoming weaker. This is a trap because over the years, the cycle continues and they keep adapting. This weakens the eye's ability to adapt to changing circumstances, such as light and distance. If we rely on glasses, it is best to only use them as needed for a time, until the prescription improves, or they are no longer needed at all.

Sunglasses are detrimental to vision. The eyes were created to spend most of their time outdoors in natural light. Sunglasses filter out life giving sun, which the eyes convert into vitamin D. Also, our rods and cones require full spectrum light to "recharge" so that we can see colors accurately and process night vision. If sunglasses are worn, they recharge at different ratios or not enough in general, so our eyes will be more sensitive to some colors than others. If we wear sunglasses constantly, without them we will need to squint to keep sunlight out. This creates tension and impairs vision. Vision should always be relaxed and fluid. Breathe into the eye sockets and feel the muscles relax. Consciously avoid squinting and allow the pupils to dilate as they were designed to do.

Please close your eyes for a moment. Do you feel the small eye muscles grabbing? Breathe and notice. Just keep them closed until the grabbing ceases, breathe, and open them again. Repeat the process. This is just to get the mind aware of what the muscles are doing. Once you learn to feel tension in the eyes, you can learn to relax the eyes.

Like any other part of the body, the eyes require healthy fuel to function properly. Overall health and alkalinity of the body is important to keep the eyes in good shape, so that they can metabolize sunlight efficiently.

So remember, eye muscles are not "weak." They are one of the most efficient muscles in the body. They just need to be "retrained" to work at sending and receiving messages from the brain. This can be done by *tracing figure 8 shapes in space or on a wall*, by *tracing the outline of certain complex objects*, or by *covering one eye, holding a detailed object (like a brush, or a pen with writing on it), and moving that object further and closer while focusing on it with the open eye.*

The human eye was designed to maintain a relatively small point of focus, and to jump around constantly to build the entire picture out of these parts; to flow from focal point to focal point. As you watch someone cross the street, for instance, instead of watching their whole body, try to allow your eyes to flow from their face, to their ear, to their neck, for example, then trace the whole form quickly. At first this may feel like a learned skill, but it may be the way we saw the world as children.

Again, our eyes thrive outdoors looking middle to far distances. We spend most of our lives indoors looking at things from a close distance, fixated on monitors, books, etc. Our eyes are not malfunctioning, they have just adapted insistently to our new lifestyle. This understanding alone can be a very powerful vision improvement tool!

Also, by noticing how our vision works, we gain access to powerful metaphors about how we see life. For instance: do we see the big picture, or do we focus on little details? Do we gaze out into the distance, or stare at the ground two feet in front of us? Do we adapt easily as we change our point of focus, or does the shift take time?

Animals are great for studying the concept of fluid vision. Notice how they never squint or strain to see. When the sun is blinding, they close their eyes partially and gently allow their pupils dilate. They seem to smile in the sun.

During healing work, people often ask me how I know where to touch.

"Because I am looking," I reply.

I think they often expect a more mystical answer. I guess I don't have one. Nothing is more mystical than observing without judgment.

"Love is the absence of judgment." - The Dalai Lama.

But perhaps "looking" for me means something different. For me it means being in the body, pulsing in the heart, flowing from moment to moment while feeling out into the universe with not only the eyes but with our whole being. This is what vision is.

Training Suggestion:

1. **Vision Awareness Exercise**

   Close your eyes for a moment. Take a deep breath. Reach up gently and touch the eyelids with your fingertips. Press a little harder now. Are your eyes soft and fluid, or hard and rigid? Massage them as needed. Gently remind them to soften. Be grateful for the gift of sight. Send love to your eyes; to all of the beauty that they allow you to witness.
   Rigid ways of thinking, being, and seeing can effect vision. Now open your eyes and see. Notice subtleties in color and shadow. Trace a complex organic form with your eyes. Now trace a geometric form. Notice the way vision works. Notice how magical it is.

   Through it all, remember to breathe into the abdomen, deep regular breaths, and blink. I can guarantee you that when your vision seizes up, breathing becomes shallow or stops. Re-learning to see is re-learning to be, and being is about breath.

Cornerstones of Clear Vision

- Breathe regularly (often when vision blurs, we'll notice that our breath has become shallow or ceased)
- Blink lightly and constantly (this moistens and massages the eyes)
- Notice tension in the eyes and allow it to pass away
- Relax the eyes and trust in your vision. Trust that you are seeing what is meant to be seen. By not squinting or straining, we retrain the pupils to dilate as needed. Trying to see impairs vision.
- Eye exercises as needed
- Wear glasses only as needed if at all
- Avoid sunglasses
- Get natural light
- Limit staring at screens. Move your eyes around often. Allow them to shift and adapt to new circumstances. Celebrate your fluid vision. Screens emit electromagnetic radiation, work with refresh rates that tire our eyes and put us in a trance state (this has been researched extensively by the advertising industry), and lock our eyes into one way of viewing.
- Super-hydrate and detoxify your body (this helps maintain fluidity in the eyes, and allows them to self-cleanse effectively).
- Clarify your goals for the future. This clarifies vision!
- Conversely, gaze into the distance with your eyes. This will help you become clear about your future! And it helps your eyes adapt to a wide range of circumstances, as they were designed to do.

Be the Change

...

"Be the change you wish to see in the world." - Gandhi.

One of the most powerful tools for facilitating change is, I think, serving as an example for others, or becoming what we wish others were. Any other approach lacks integrity and creates stress in our bodies and minds. Caroline Myss postulates that Integrity and Honor are two of the most important components of maintaining a healthy energetic system. If we fall out of integrity, our immune system suffers and we lose the foundation upon which to build joyous, fulfilling lives.

If we expect others to flow with us, to not harbor resentment and anger, and to live each moment in celebration, we can help them by becoming fluid in our own body and mind. Moving loosely, happily, lovingly through the world can loosen up those we come into contact with. Like joy, fluidity is contagious.

We breathe and they breathe. It is an unconscious process that the body goes through; mirroring those around us. As societal creatures, we long to belong. Smiles are contagious. So are posture, beauty, and positive thoughts.

As I sit in the DMV, I ground myself, plant my feet, and send positive thoughts to a mother with grocery bags. She seems overwhelmed by her frantic child crawling under chairs. I just radiated love, without judgment. Within minutes, she softens. She turns her head toward the child, with a soft face, and almost smiles. She sets down her judgments; loosens her "grip." And, because he no longer feels the need to struggle for freedom, he comes to sit beside her. I'd think it was a miracle but I do this often now. It is me playing in the hologram.

"Whatever you think the world is withholding from you, you are withholding from the world." - Eckhart Tolle

What might you be withholding from the world right now? What might you be holding on to that may not be serving you?

What would releasing it mean? How would it show up in your life?

Chasing Buddha

● ● ●

I am running through Elk Grove, just south of Sacramento. This area is very underdeveloped in some places. There are vast swathes of grassland, untended orchards, and swamps with ancient, leafless oaks that twist up into the sky. Miniature rivers, some mere trickles, gingerly wind through the landscape.

There's a chill in the air, as winter clings to her throne. I love this time of year; the incipience of spring. Fruit trees flowering everywhere remind me of Japanese woodblock prints. This is me thinking. I keep reminding myself to just be. A Hiroshige print of plum blossoms springs to mind.

I think of how I came to this place. It was by accident. We were going to go up to Alaska, my girlfriend and I, and the plan got sidetracked, so we settled here where she grew up. After a few of our back up plans also fell through, we decided to call this place home for a time. There's nothing out here. It's at the periphery of where I want to be. I visited once years ago when I lived in San Francisco, en route to Sacramento, and I remember thinking: "What do people do out here?"

"There are no accidents," I remind myself, gently.

As I run, a new affirmation runs through my head. I speak it aloud when my determination wanes:

"I trust in the process of life. I am safe."

How irrational fears keep us from reaching our full potential. As I slip into fearful thinking, my legs begin to ache and I gasp for air. I crank up the affirmation, and remind myself that all is well. The pain subsides a little each time I say it with conviction.

I watch my mind waver. As I let it run its course, watching it without judgment, a dialog ensues:

"Why are you here?" it says. "In the middle of nowhere. It's a dead end. There's nothing out here but brown grass and old farm houses. You know this isn't your destiny, yet you can't afford to move. Even your relationship is falling apart. You're trapped out here! Admit it!"

I smile, because I know how clever the mind chatter can be. As I crunch along a narrow dirt path, a flock of geese fly over in a perfect V. It's an arrow, pointing to the present moment.

"Thank you for sharing, mind chatter." I say. "I'm here now, so I might as well be fully present and enjoy it. There is so much beauty here. The brown grass really brings out the blue in the sky."

A variation on this theme keeps playing as I approach the 8 mile mark. I hit a wall. My left calf is seizing up. I allow the run to taper off into a walk.

I think of the marathon monks, the Lung-gom-pa monks in Tibet, and in Japan the monks of Mount Hiei, who run endless hours on scant nourishment, in minimal footwear, chanting mantras, chasing Buddha. I wonder if they hit walls?

They must. They're monks, but they're human. The mantras bring them closer to their full potential. The Tibetans write something on their feet in Sanskrit that lends them superhuman legs and thunderous hearts.

I wonder how that works? It's impossible for a monk shod in sandals to run 52 miles a day for three months in a row, subsisting on little bowls of grain. My mind starts rebelling.

"Grain is hardly a food at all," it says. "It's not possible. Maybe they slip in something else? It's almost by accident that grain became the human staple. Man can't live on bread alone."

There's that word again. "Accident." I start jogging again. What does that word even mean? To me it means not taking responsibility... not "trusting in the process of life."

These monks are expressing their full potential, because they believe in what they're doing. They're literally chasing their dreams without hesitation. It is I who am letting my mind hold me back by being skeptical of them. I am not here by accident. This is not a land of nowhere. And if they run for days on end, I can make it home.

"The things which are impossible with men are possible with God" - Luke 18:27

I gradually increase my speed until I'm sprinting. I can tell people in cars are watching me. I wonder what they're thinking; if they're inspired, annoyed? I sprint for what seems like miles, nourished by only the pure potentiality and the gut wrenching beauty that's always surrounding me but I rarely get to see. I get winded as my own heart thunders in my ribs, my joints creek, and my nose whistles. But my body adapts, and I find a fast stride that feels natural and liquid, like these flowing streams. I smile into the sun.

As I stumble up to the house I'm staying in, I notice that it's beginning to look more like a home.

"I'm manifesting my own destiny with every step, with every breath, with every word," I tell myself, opening the door.

Sex and Sacred Intimacy

...

Quantum mechanics, the holographic nature of the universe, karma. These doctrines are by no means simple, but they are fathomable. Love, on the other hand, is life's great mystery. How many great men and women have been rendered powerless by the simple, ethereal gaze of their beloved? How many fortunes have been thrown away and vast empires toppled?

We rush into love and wonder what we've done. We finally get out and loneliness descends. It can be a frustrating escapade. And yet, coldly and calculatingly attempting to avoid love's perils never works. Suffering comes when we make the mistake of thinking that all of our love must emanate from and toward one being. Love is all around us. Intimacy is all around us. So let's narrow down the focus slightly for the moment. What we are speaking about here is sexual, soul bonded love.

Accepting love as the great mystery brings some peace, some solace. It may also bring some relief in the long run (though probably not in the moment) when we realize that the purpose of intimate relationships is not comfort or joy, but transformation and growth. Our soul mates bring us to new, higher vibrational levels of being. When we expect happiness, joy, and ease, and those things are not delivered, chaos ensues. When we are open to what love brings, the suffering and the rapture, love can bring us ever more.

Sexual intimacy can be one of the climaxes of the human condition. It can also be a degrading, addictive energy leech.

When we clear our patterns from the past, it opens us up to choose lovers that empower us to fulfill greater and greater potential. What a thrill it is to share life with a kindred spirit!

Many of us perpetually recapitulate the relationships we had with our parents, or the relationship they had with each other.

I noticed in the past that my relationships began to look like my mother's relationship to my father. Like clockwork, I would fall head over heels, become ecstatic, allow my partner to idealize me, and then imprison myself by orchestrating the whole situation so that I resided with them and was struggling financially. It was frustrating to both my partners and I.

Now that I have cleared that pattern, through various trauma release work, transformational bodywork, and simple awareness, I am free to love whom I choose, and much more open to receiving love.

Each body is different. Learning the anatomy of human beings in general, and of our partner specifically, allows us to pleasure one another in sacred ways.

Again, self love is the key to fulfilling relationships. People who harbor an abundance of critical thoughts about the self will always look to another to fulfill them. In this place of poverty consciousness, it is difficult for love to flourish. It is like a flower growing out of the sidewalk, getting trampled every time it blooms again.

Sexual energy is some of the most powerful creative energy we have at our disposal. Ancient tantric practitioners learned to channel the natural desire for pleasure into their quest for spiritual actualization. Napoleon Hill, in 1937, wrote of using sexual energy to facilitate the pursuit of monetary wealth in his now famous Think and Grow Rich.

Inspiration enters our crown chakra at the top of our head and trickles down through our body for processing and manifestation. We can throw that energy away in various ways before the manifestation can occur. One way is through careless speech. If we continually speak about our plans or our alchemical journey, we lose our power as the inspiration, that source energy, leaks out of Vishuddha, our throat chakra.

Likewise, we can squander the energy by expelling it through Svadisthana, our 2nd or sacral chakra, by way of sex. Semen is pure creative power and contains unlimited potential. The miracle of life is that we are able to procreate and send other powerful little creators out into the world like dandelion spores to fulfill their destiny. When we throw our seed away carelessly, through masturbation and meaningless sex, not only do we lose life force and a finite vital essence that cannot be replaced, we also squander our creative abilities.

If we use sex in the hopes of bolstering self worth, we lose. We continually throw away our life force toward anyone who will take it, or anyone who is somewhat appealing, in the hopes that they will make us feel more worthy of our own lives. The irony is that when we do this, we diminish a finite life essence and our integrity, which can lead to premature aging, depression, a lack of energy, etc. We also send a message to the universe that we will settle for less than we deserve.

It is said in Taoism that when a man has an orgasm externally, 1/3 of his energy the next day goes to replenishing his store of seeds.

So should we give up sex and become celibate? Not necessarily.

First, we can choose empowering partners; partners that help us grow and thrive. Keep your heart peeled for kindred spirits. The more interaction we have with our soul contracts, the more likely we are to fulfill our destiny. The more time we spend with others, the more convoluted our journey becomes and the less soul contracts we are able to fulfill.

Second, we can remain conscious through the whole ordeal, from the courtship to the point of orgasm to the separation. The moment of orgasm is the closest many of us ever come to the joy of pure being. We can learn tantric practices to expand on this potential. I like to take a deep abdominal breath at the point of orgasm. We often hold our breath when we sustain great pain. It is ironic that this conditioning trickles over into moments of intense pleasure. Breathe and feel the ecstasy.

Third, we men can learn to preserve our seed and universal creative energy. There are ways to redirect an orgasm inward, into a higher chakra. In this way, the epicurean pleasure of sex can still be enjoyed, and the life essence is not thrown away in the process. In fact, it is fortified. Lost life essence can create bitterness and pain when it becomes a power struggle. The man, overly drained, can become like a frightened tiger whose instincts take over.

Some women delight at seeing the seed spill out at the moment of climax, and some men delight in depositing it here or there. This is fine, but we can ask ourselves if this is love or the love of power? Do we love the other or are we merely conquering them? Conquer the self and allow the love to flow.

In precious moments we can follow our intuition and know playfulness, passion, ecstasy, when it stems from a place of respect and deep love.

In the realm of sacred intimacy, vulnerability is power. When we refuse to be vulnerable, we can never drink deeply of the nectar of love. We are like hummingbirds, frantically flitting about, stealing a thimble's worth of sweetness from every flower. When we actually slow down in the presence of one, and reach out with our whole being, trembling, we take a risk. We give up the other flowers in the field for the moment; we set them free. We have dared to dream the impossible dream of love, and the universe hears our dream and delights in it.

Love begins to rise up all around us, in the guise of miracles; but these aren't "miracles" per say. Our eyes are just adjusting to the new world, as if to a blinding light. Mortals wrapped in love begin to appear in the street, on the subway, on the beach. There is nowhere we can hide where they will not find us, as we've summoned them by the thunderous power of our vulnerability. Vulnerability is moving through fear to a frontier beyond our edge. Once we are there, we can breathe into the eyes of the other, merge with the other, love the other.

It is not whether we are afraid of vulnerability or not; we *all* are. That is what vulnerability means. It comes from the Latin, vulnerare, or wound, so it means "prone to being wounded." Where's the joy in that? Where's the rapture? They are hiding where we've least suspected to look; at the heart of vulnerability.

It takes removing our armor for another to penetrate our essence. With moist eyes or a tremulous voice we say: "My heart is yours. Yours to celebrate, worship, possess, cradle; yours to shatter, lock away, use, own. Your definition of love is yours, as is my heart."

"And I would choose to be with you
If the choice were mine to make
But you can make decisions too
And you can have this heart to break."
- Billy Joel

Training Suggestions:

1. Biodynamic Centering Practice

This practice trains us to feel the physical and emotional lure of another.

Sit or stand quietly for a moment, in front of a partner. Look into each others' eyes for a moment. Take deep, abdominal breaths.

Notice their beauty, and where that beauty resonates in you. Notice their vulnerability, and where that makes you tremble. Notice where you may be projecting.

Again, call to your awareness the three spheres; the one in the head, the heart, and the navel. They are referred to as the three sisters: Nina, Wowa, and Lola, because using the sounds as mantras can activate those centers.

Remember to keep the three sisters in vertical alignment. With the eyes open, where do you feel the pull toward your partner? Instead of gazing into the soul of him, try pulling your attention back, and placing it midway between the two of you. Where do you feel it now?

Now close the eyes and breathe deeply. See if you can come back into your midline, or if there is still a pull. Just notice and be aware.

Ideally, we can maintain our midline and our selves even in the presence of another. When we feel a physical or energetic lean in the direction of another, we can back up and regain our composure. We are then free to pursue sacred intimacy, which is a direct gateway to self knowledge (Intimacy = into me I see).

2. White Tantric Gaze

A monk taught me this practice when I was having difficulty with a partner. He called it "White Tantric Yoga."
Sit comfortably across from your partner, cross legged with the knees almost touching. Now, take one another's hands gently, with the left hand always on top of the right, which helps scramble our dominant patterns.

Now gaze into the eyes of your partner. Take deep abdominal breaths. Notice what is going on in your body while you look into their eyes with love. Notice the voice, the aches, and the sensations. Just notice them as they arise and pass.

Move beyond the discomfort. We spend so much time speaking, fidgeting, moving, heeding our mind chatter, making love, leaping from task to task, day to day, and defending ourselves all along the way. This practice puts us back in touch with the essence of our partner. Continue for three to ten minutes, or until you both soften or until one of you surrenders.

This can be a valuable practice for maintaining a relationship, restructuring an ailing one, or beginning a new one in a powerful and compelling way. When we simply share the mystery and beauty of one another without judgment, love rises to the surface of our experience. We remember the reasons we chose this person. We regain clarity on what we need now, in this precious moment.

Recommended Reading:

Cultivating Male Sexual Energy by M. Chia
The Anatomy of the Spirit by Caroline Myss

Soul Contracts: Unlocking the Sacred Mystery of Love

• • •

One powerful love connection arises out of a soul contract. The universe is constantly orchestrating the matrix so that we continually come into contact with people that facilitate us learning the life lessons that we've chosen to master. This makes for a fulfilling and transformational life experience.

Have you ever met someone that overwhelmed your senses and rational mind, and just plowed their way into your life? Perhaps you and them had / have a soul contract?

In this model, when someone appears powerfully in your life, it is because there are unresolved issues between the two of you. Taking this awareness into relationships can provide greater clarity and can make it easier to accept difficult situations. The recent film "Cloud Atlas" explores this concept in a compelling way.

A certain mystery is inherent in this model. We catch glimpses of clarity now and then, but there will always be things that are beyond understanding. If it weren't that way, the soul journey through the flesh would serve no purpose. The lessons are lessons because we discover them as we move through them. Though some people actually do recall past lives in vivid detail, it is fairly rare. Most of us just get fleeting premonitions. Those that do recall them often have great difficulty integrating this awareness into their current life.

Understanding patterns often involves tracing their roots back to childhood, and sometimes back to past lives. This is a critical feature of my own healing and my own work. I also love to sit in idle reverie and ponder the idea.

May I share another segment of the saga regarding the previous lover who became enamored with a woman?

Throughout our relationship, I noticed that, though I loved her deeply, we seemed to be moving in different directions, on different paths, and at different paces. Due to our partnership, neither of us seemed to be expressing our full potential. Our love, sexual chemistry, and possibly a dose of denial and fear held us together by the skin of our teeth.

Then it happened, the prelude to a classic tale... my lover fell in love with someone else.

Since the problem was posed as "If I stay I create problems, and if I truly love her I will leave," I left, with some resistance.

After the anger and confusion passed, and I spent time lying in bed, facing my own fear and anger until they dissipated, I began to reframe the experience in another way, more empowering way. It was an "accident."

My partner's new obsession burst into our lives like a torrential force of nature. I was angry first at my lover, and then at her lover. 'How could she do this to me?' I thought. 'Throw away everything we shared for a fling? How could anyone be so selfish... so reckless?!'

Over time, the feeling dulled but I still felt tension arise when I thought about them together, wrapped in each others' arms.

While I was lying in bed in my new temporary abode, I reached over and my fingers found a book that evidently belonged to my roommate: *Spiritual Psychology* by Steve Rother. I thumbed through and opened the book to a section on "bump" contracts.

According to the author, we often negotiate with another soul before this life, so that if we ever get too far off course, and things begin looking dire, this other soul will graciously come in, as if on cue, and "bump" us back on course. Interestingly, the "bump" often comes in the form of an irresistible, usually short-term attraction. This is called a "bump contract."

I sighed and shuddered. That's how I knew something in me was released. Once the experience was reframed in this way (by a serendipitous brush with my roommate's book), I can honestly say that I now look on this other woman with swells of gratitude. She did me a great service and I will be forever grateful to her, and whatever compassionate force put that book next to my bed that day.

Now the logical mind may chime in here and ask: Excuse me, but can we actually verify the existence of soul contracts, other than an intuitive knowing? Probably not. However, after shifting my viewpoint, I was able to release my anger and confusion and shift to a mindset of gratitude. It was a powerful, "accidental" reframe (an NLP technique) and I have used similar techniques many times since.

Beliefs are always a choice, and we can choose beliefs that empower us.

I used to believe that we lived in a cold if mathematically precise universe, at the whims of forces beyond our understanding, and that people evolved on Earth by chance and circumstance, and simply survived and attempted to procreate because these were evolutionary, biological imprints. Birth was either planned or accidental, and health decayed until death, when our cellular energy was recycled into the earth.

Now I believe that we live in a safe and loving universe, the Earth is a living entity, and souls flow in and out of our lives at destined times as we grow and evolve to become complete beings. When we "die" we ascend or reincarnate into a new phase of our spiritual evolution. Life is a stream of synchronistic occurrences, all orchestrated by us in collaboration with higher powers, for the sake of our spiritual evolution and fulfillment.

All of our life is a story. When we begin to realize that we create the story, we engage the shaman's power to write our own destinies. When we lose a love, we can become embittered and lose faith in love entirely, or thank them for the time together, the precious moments, and the growth. We can wallow in the abyss of despair or we can allow that experience to inspire new creations. The event never changed; we did. This is our power.

I used to rebel against the past life doctrine because it was impossible to validate. Now I work and live from a place of allowing, and marvel at the beautiful experiences that continue to arise and mystify me.

Fluidity in Love

• • •

We are born of water, in water, fluid beings. When the "water breaks" and we emerge into the world, we "think" that we become more and more "solid." The truth is, we remain fluid, and our bodies are still more water than anything else. Water is the universal conduit, and also provides the metaphor for an empowering way of being. We can choose to remain fluid and flow in each moment.

"Be like water." – Bruce Lee

"Nothing in the world
is as soft and yielding as water.
Yet for dissolving the hard and inflexible,
nothing can surpass it." – Tao Te Ching (Stephen Mitchell Translation)

Fluidity, for me, means being open to the present moment in every area of life; in work, in friendship, in play, and in love. Holding onto events from the past, and turning them over and over in our minds, creates patterns that effect our actions moment to moment.

Also, in the vast fluid intelligence system that is our body, holding onto things mentally and emotionally is holding onto them physically as well. We experience "stiffness" in our bodies, pain, dis-ease, when we are unable to release something that no longer serves us.

When we hold onto a past lover, for instance, our heart is not fully open to new love. Can you see how this might be true? Try as we may to trust, unconscious fear has us close our hearts and hide our vulnerability. We are in the grips of fear and fear is antithetical to love. When two people are this way, defense mechanisms clash and chaos can ensue.

Can you relate?

May I share a personal story?

I once became enamored with a woman who was absolutely perfect in my mind (story), and I was thrilled that after months of courting we shared a few nights of profound connection. However, when that passed, and family issues arose that rendered her unavailable for a relationship, I desperately clung to those early memories, instead of listening to my heart in the present and giving this lovely creature the space she craved. It strained our love.

Have you experienced this?

Now, after reeling from that experience and trying every strategy my mind could think of to reconcile with her, I finally let go, released her from my body (between the third and fourth rib), and allowed myself to be open to new possibilities again.

I came into my body, and just allowed myself to feel grateful for her, so grateful, without attachment. With this momentous vibrational shift, she began to contact me again, and instead of idealizing her and surging in, this time we were able to meet, in passion, but also grounded, with a foundation that had potential to last.

Now I help my clients unravel similar experiences as they move toward wholeness and deep love.

We all deserve happiness, it is our birthright. And returning to fluidity, in body and mind, allows us to open our hearts to the present moment, sing our soul songs and attract our soul mates from the far corners of the earth.

When we are all in this vibration, nothing can keep us apart. We sing our soul songs and dance toward one another in a cosmic dance that shatters reality and creates legends.

Pain as the Path to Joy

• • •

Physical pain often represents "feelings" being stored until the mind is ready to process them; until they can be fully "felt". Fully feeling from moment to moment when sensations arise helps prevent trauma being stored in our field.

Healing trauma becomes much easier as we begin to understand a little more about why the body does what it does.

When our body undergoes trauma that it feels is too intense for our mind to deal with, it stores it in the cellular tissue, for future processing. It can become what John Upledger calls an "energy cyst." Over time, this pocket of unprocessed energy can have devastating effects on vital organs and tissues, depending on its location. For instance, falling on your tail bone can effect digestive organs years later. The harder the impact, the deeper into the tissues the energy cyst penetrates.

Emotions can also find their way into the cellular tissue and remain there. The body wants to release them, so it gives signs; aches and pains. The mind tends to shrug it off as something merely physical. We can get massages and adjustments, *and the pain will keep returning until it is linked to the original source; what I call the seed source*. Then it can be fully released and healed.

Since trauma release is a portion of the work that I specialize in, it is perhaps easier to illustrate with a case study.

Lucy and her Father

• • •

Lucy (*name changed for anonymity*) was in her early twenties. She came to me complaining of a vague pain and a lack of mobility in both of her shoulders, as well as an "inability to cry." She wondered if she "felt enough." Even at her father's funeral, she said, she hadn't cried at all. These were signs that this might be a session focused on healing trauma.

I begin to work gently around her body, getting to know how it moves and how it responds to me, my energy. To men, to people in general. Some of us are very guarded. This work can be done standing or lying down. In this case I lie her down on a cushion and we begin the exploration. I guide her into deep, abdominal breaths as I gently take her arm rotate it at the shoulder joint. She has complained about her shoulder but that's not why I'm there. I see something. Usually what a client thinks is the issue is not. As I rotate the shoulder, I notice that the breath halts and her forehead furrows just slightly. It is so subtle that I almost gloss over it.

I return the arm to that position again and give a persistent tug. Lucy is frozen.

She becomes a child in the hologram. I don't know how to explain this phenomenon, but I see it. Her face, her entire body regresses in time, back to the source of her trauma. It was once too subtle for me to witness. Now it seems obvious.

"Take a deep breath," I say. She hesitates, and then tries to get away with a very shallow breath.

"One more time," I say, smiling. "A little deeper."

As the breath floods her lungs, there is a shudder and a rush of tears. I allow them to flow for a moment; to cleanse her.

"Where did you go?" I ask.

"My father passed away about a year ago," she replies. "And I never cried. He used to pull me by that arm when I was young, to cross the street."

So little Lucy had connected the tissues around the gleno-humeral joint to her deceased father. When we made this connection, and she was able to emote, the shoulder stiffness and pain vanished. Will it ever return? The honest answer is, it may. But with the new awareness, it may not, or it may pass quickly. It no longer holds Lucy in its bonds. Healing has never been a point in time; it is a process, an unraveling. Sometimes a healing is delivered with a beautiful cure. Sometimes not. Either way, the world around us transforms.

Healing trauma can have far reaching effects. I like to say that our lives are like a hologram, and adjusting one area can ripple out into all areas of our life. Having released her emotions about her father, Lucy was able to begin to trust men again. She was married a few months later to a man whom she had been with for years but had been unable to fully commit to.

There really are only two emotions; Love and Fear.

Healing trauma involves releasing emotional baggage. This allows us to overcome our fears of repeating the past; in essence, to fear less and love more.

Feet: Our Energetic Roots

• • •

Our feet are the foundation of our physical life. All that we are, physically, arises from our feet. Our feet root us to the earth, and allow us to stand on our toes and touch the sky. Our feet carry us all of our days, from the first moment we are able to walk, to the last.

So much can be ascertained about us by our feet; how we carry ourselves through the world, our self conception, our energetic health, our accident history, etc.

The feet are masterpieces of engineering. These 26 bones articulate in subtle ways to help us move gracefully through our lives. Non-fluid ways of thinking and standing can keep this grand design from functioning optimally, but in our full power, our feet flex and move in a myriad of ways, allowing us to adapt to a broad range of circumstances and terrain.

Look down for a moment. Do you love your feet?

Most shoes hinder the natural evolution of the foot. The foot is designed to flex gracefully and cushion impact as we move through space time. When we wear shoes with thick, cushioned souls, we can lose touch with our feet. We begin to walk without awareness, landing heavily on our heels, sending stress vectors shooting up our legs into our knees, our hips, our back.

Through coaching, massage, and joint manipulation, many issues commonly thought to be "genetic" can be remedied. Sometimes a simple shift of awareness can make a dramatic difference.

As our feet become beautiful again, our health and vitality will follow as meridians in our toes reawaken.

The toes are perfectly evolved to support us in balancing our bodies through a host of mercurial circumstances. We dance, run, leap, walk, crouch, creep, reach, tip toe. The Asian acupuncture meridians flow down our legs and run down each toe. Planting the toes on the earth allows earth energy to flow into the meridians. It also allows us to release physical and emotional stress out through our energetic and physical system. The toes are like energetic exhaust points.

After the millions of steps we take in each lifetime, the cumulative energy needs somewhere to go. Standing on the ball of the foot, with the toes raised, can cause issues such as bone spurs and neuroma. Going against the grain of our bodies' natural design causes suffering.

Training Suggestions:

1. Fluid Standing Tutorial

Remove your shoes and stand upright. Imagine three spheres the size of oranges in your body; one in your skull, one in your heart, and one in your belly, below your belly button. Take a deep breath into your abdomen and allow these spheres to line up. Take a deep breath again through the nose and exhale through your mouth. Notice any tension in your face, your neck, your shoulders, or your chest. On each exhale, release, and sink deeper into relaxation.
Stand with the feet parallel, about hip width apart.

Where a joint is locked, energy cannot flow. Soften the knees by bending them slightly.

Our toes are designed to balance us. Spread your toes as wide as you can. Feel them on the ground. The large toe supports the foot in maintaining a healthy arch. An arch collapses when we cave in on ourselves. It is not genetic, though we do learn ways of being from our relatives and those around us.

The small toe helps keep the feet from turning outward. At first it may be an effort to spread the small toe. Just do your best. If it helps, place a cotton ball between the toes and see how that feels.

2. Barefoot Awareness Practice

Again, remove your shoes and socks and look down at your feet. If you can, stand on the earth or in the grass. As you breathe into your abdomen, imagine red roots growing down from your perineum, through your legs, through your feet and down into the core of the earth.

Have you loved your feet? Breathe and be aware of the volume of your feet. Move your awareness to each toe and see if you can feel it. Wiggle them. Celebrate them.

Close the eyes and breathe. Open them and breathe. Do you have stories about your feet? Just notice and be aware.

Hugs and the Lure of Human Connection

• • •

Hugs cure. They are a healthy exchange of human energy. Bodies transfer what they need to one another, and the powerful flow of two overlapping auras throws off the excess. Hugs strengthen the immune system, decrease depression, and help with a host of ailments. They also feel good and facilitate healthy human connection.

When we hug with our heads to the right, our hearts share energy. Heart to heart hugs perform better in muscle tests.

When we hug with our heads to the left, we share liver energy. This is something to be aware of. The liver is not only full of chemical toxins, but also emotional toxins, such as anger and rage.

Training Suggestion

1. Conscious Embrace

Look gently into the eyes of the other for a moment. Take a breath and allow time to gauge whether an embrace will be appropriate in this moment. If so, move in.

Place your arms around the other, with your head to over their left shoulder. Close your eyes and just hold. Allow your abdomens to touch. Breathe into each other. Feel the love, the joy. Many of us have only ever given and received awkward hugs just for the sake of decorum. Conscious hugs heal.

After three to five deep breaths, give a slight squeeze and release gently. Allow them to flow back into their own lives. Since life is a series of embracing and letting go, hugs are an ideal time to practice this concept.

When I was a Headless Monk

• • •

I have a story. We all have stories. We are constantly creating, revising, and embellishing our stories in each moment. Whether something is "true" or not remains to be seen. When someone says "everything happens for the best," we may think "Really? How do you know?"

The raw answer is we can't know, logically. Empirical data may never arrive to satiate us. How can it? We cannot know how an alternate course of action might have changed our life for the better or for the worse. However, though we cannot know with our minds, we can know with our bodies. We can feel what resonates with our physical structure. Once we catch that glimpse, we can decide to believe. We can reframe the situation so that it empowers us, by altering our story. Even if nothing changes in the chain of events, we can revise the meaning we give to the story. This is everything.

I have a story about a past life and how it had been leaking out over and over again in the form of a persistent pattern. May I share it with you?

It is not an easy story to tell, because I pieced it together at random intervals and through a synchronistic chain of events.

All of my life I have been fascinated by monks, particularly Zen monks. When I was in my mid-twenties, I briefly toyed with the notion of becoming a monk. The idea enraged my partner at the time, understandably. I visited most of the temples in Kyoto and I felt so at peace wandering the grounds. It was difficult to leave. It felt like home.

Eight years later, during a past life regression session, I had a vision of myself as a monk in Japan in the eighteenth century. I was unconditionally devoted to my mentor, who was approximately the same age as me. For this reason, he was still hanging around in my energy field as a dark presence in this lifetime.

You may recall that I broke my neck, cracked my 5th cervical vertebrate in an ocean incident in 2008. While a powerful practitioner was palpating the bones, I had flashbacks of the ocean, and she saw a flash of me being beheaded with a sword, for the sake of my mentor. I gave my life for him.

I carried this story of needing a figure to be unconditionally devoted to for many years. Evidently, in the 18th century I had not made an empowering choice, since the figure turned out to be a dark presence. The story is not as valuable as the understanding. The breakthrough came when I realized that the pattern was perpetuating itself in a place I might not have suspected: through my love affairs.

I would choose a woman, or, more accurately, a woman would be placed in my path by circumstance, and I would make the decision to be unconditionally devoted to her. Once the object of my devotion was decided upon, virtually nothing could drive me away; not abuse, violence, unfaithfulness, distance, suffering. I set as stoic as a monk in the presence of my "beloved." And life without an object of devotion felt incomplete and foreign.

Once I pieced this riddle together, through random fragments of life experience, and gently witnessing clues, I felt the story lighten its grip on me. When I feel the impulse to unconditionally give myself to someone, I can detach myself from the story and remember how that particular pattern had shown up in the past and there was evidence that it didn't work.
However, one person I could unconditionally devote myself to was... myself. Anyone else could be subject to corruption and human fallacy. In any case, anyone else was a projection of myself anyway.

Loving the self unconditionally can transform our world with no side effects. We merely bloom to fill the beautiful space around us with more of what we truly are; more of our essence.

Loving ourselves allows us to love others completely.

So stories came to me, as stories come, and I framed them so that they served me. Was I a Japanese monk in the eighteenth century? I have no way of knowing, but I have chosen to believe and this has enriched my life and empowered me to experience ever greater joy, love, and understanding.

Transforming the Mundane into Sacred Ritual: The Power of Imagination

• • •

We can continue to grow mentally for the rest of our days, or we can peak and descend ever downward, as I once considered doing.

As we become illuminated, we can use every experience that we lure into our lives as a tool for growth. The world becomes our training ground.

We spend so much time doing dishes, laundry, cooking, cleaning, driving, eating. Since our mind creates our reality, and visualizations hold untold power, we can continually use that power to our benefit.

As Zen monks sweep the temple steps, they are not only sweeping the temple steps; they are sweeping the dust of "unconsciousness" out of their minds. As they weed a garden, they are uprooting unnatural thoughts from their consciousness. Buddha suggests that as you're releasing wastes from your body, imagine that you are purging negative thoughts from your mind. While I run I often imagine that I am approaching a physical goal. I also imagine my chakras as pinwheels that spin in the wind as I gain momentum.

As we remember that our imagination is not distinct from reality, vast resources open up to us. We enter into "trance" states many times throughout the day. We can harness the power of these naturally occurring states in order to retrain the unconscious mind.

The next time you are doing the dishes, sweeping the floor, or mowing the lawn and someone asks you what's taking so long, you can reply that you are training for enlightenment and enlightenment takes time.

Fluid Movement

...

Developing physical strength and aerobic stamina helps us live in flow. Someone who is aerobically fit has up to 25% more blood than someone who is not. The body creates more blood in order to deliver more oxygen more effectively to the tissues in need. And strong, flexible muscles allow us to move with grace and balance.

I am a proponent of what I like to call fluid running. Did you know that, when it comes to distance, a human can out run any animal on Earth? Even a horse. Native American Indians would chase down horses and simply catch them when they fell in exhaustion. I advocate running in barefoot or minimalist footwear in a fluid way because this brings us in touch with our body and our energy system. This applies to running and also to walking and life in general. Thick, cushioned shoes bring us out of touch with our bodies and make us less conscious. It is difficult to calibrate exactly where our foot is, and to compensate our body often needs to make subtle shifts that solve the issue in the moment but can create dis-ease in the long term.

Running is one example of fluid movement that I prize for its simplicity. I've also studied Chen Tai Chi and various schools of Yoga and learned a great deal from each.

Fluid movement involves moving toward something (future) while remaining exquisitely embodied (present). In this way it becomes the perfect metaphor for life itself.

Ideally, every movement we ever make should be fluid; not only physically but also metaphorically, as in a transition to a new job or relationship. We can choose to move in and out of each situation, each moment with grace and flow.

Being conscious while we are in motion can give us priceless clues about where we may be holding tension in the body. When I walk, for instance, I notice that my left shoulder often rises. I consciously breathe, drop it and move along. I look on it not with judgment but with curiosity.

As I describe fluid movement and attempt to embody it, I often think of a cat. Cats move so gracefully, so softly, and yet when a cat needs to fight or flee, it becomes a dangerous creature. To witness a feline vacillate between motion and stillness so effortlessly is inspiring and beautiful to me.

If we undulate in and out of consciousness while we are moving, accidents and injuries are inevitable; not only sweeping, dramatic accidents, but stress vectors from repeated strain causing long-term damage.

As we begin to walk more consciously, we may notice that one foot falls more heavily than the other, or our elbow locks up, or one knee turns out. Being in the body in this way, during motion, forces us to remain fluid. We could not walk in such obscenely uncomfortable positions if we were fully present in our bodies.

Many of us walk hastily to "get" somewhere, as though life weren't with us on the whole journey. Feeling into this truth in every moment can be transformative. In Zen Buddhism, a walking meditation was developed, because monks would often rise after meditating and slip right into unconsciousness again, scampering off to lunch or bed. What good is meditation if it only works while we're sitting on a cushion in the lotus position?

The more we move, the more we feel, and feeling is thriving. If we can create space in our lives for fluid movement, we engage ancient biological programming, evolutionary design, and reactivate our full potential.

Life is always with us as we flow from moment to moment. Can we embrace it even as we move from here to there?

The Subtle Art of Thriving

• • •

Over the years, I've narrowed the art of Thriving down to 20 principles. Though they are each critical, I have attempted to list them in order of importance. They are a summary of much of what I have discussed throughout the book, with a few new points. I left them mildly ambiguous in the hopes that they may inspire you in unique ways.

1. *Remember to Breathe*
2. *Super Hydrate with "Sacred" Water*
3. *Eat Real "Blessed" Food*
4. *Maintain the Alkaline Balance*
5. *Cleanse Regularly*
6. *Soak in the Sun*
7. *The Body Electric A : Develop aerobic stamina. Find joyous ways to move.*
8. *The Body Electric B: Develop physical strength.*
9. *The Body Electric C: Develop flexibility; body and mind.*
10. *Schedule Adequate Dreamtime*
11. *Develop an Inspiring Inner Space*
12. *Touch Nature*
13. *Cultivate Awareness*
14. *Create an Empowering Community*
15. *Feed the Mind Forever*
16. *Learn the Language of your Soul*
17. *Clarify your Vision*
18. *Manifest Abundance*
19. *Embody your Destiny*
20. *Celebrate The Present Moment, Always*

Conclusion

...

I want to express my gratitude to you for taking the time to read these words. As we each flow into our bliss, we are transforming the world. No two people will create the same experience for themselves after reading this, or any, book. And that is the beauty of the experience.

I wish you ease and joy on your journey to wholeness, which is actually a realization of what is already there.

I like to think that the universe is rejoicing in you and I as we fearlessly seek to fully embody the full spectrum of the human experience.

We are not looking up into the skies or down into the valleys for the truth, but within.

And once we embody it, by god the world will know us by the light in our eyes!

A Penultimate Request

...

If you found value in this book, please take a moment to review it on Amazon, blog about it, recommend it to a friend, tweet it, reread it, dog ear it, sleep with it under your pillow, or share it on Facebook. May it spread across the landscape like wildflowers of illumination.

Also, I'd love to hear your stories of personal transformation and growth. Please post them in your review or email them to me through flowhealingarts.org.

If you are curious about working with me personally, on a custom transformational program, please contact me.

I look forward to growing alongside you.

About the Author

• • •

Steven Budden, H.H.W.P, H.L.C., M.B.W., M.F.A. runs Flow Healing Arts in the San Francisco Bay Area.

In addition to being a healer, he is a songwriter, visual artist, and fiction and non-fiction author .

He published The Flop Eared Gospels, a novel, in 2012.

PS. I'd like to think that you know me at least a little bit by now.

3105421R00089

Printed in Great Britain
by Amazon.co.uk, Ltd.,
Marston Gate.